CW00350022

*What's The Point
Of It All?*

Other titles in the
Scripture for Living series

What's The Point Of It All?

Damian Lundy FSC

DARTON, LONGMAN AND TODD
LONDON

First published in 1992 by
Darton, Longman and Todd Ltd
89 Lillie Road, London SW6 1UD

© 1992 Damian Lundy FSC

ISBN 0–232–51965–X

A catalogue record for this book is available
from the British Library

The Scripture quotations are taken from the
New Jerusalem Bible, published and copyright 1985 by
Darton, Longman and Todd Ltd and Doubleday & Co Inc
and used by permission of the publishers

The cover illustration, The High Plateau,
is by Elizabeth Wang

'*Much of our life might be spent in darkness
and obscurity, as God teaches us to live by
Faith: yet when He chooses, He can show
us the journey we have made with Him –
by a glimpse as though from a high plateau.*'

Phototypeset in 10/12½ pt Trump by Intype, London
Printed and bound in Great Britain
at the University Press, Cambridge

Contents

Introduction

THE WRITINGS OF THE BIBLE – the Scriptures – are the Word of God. They are of supreme importance to all Christians and to all who wish to know and understand the meaning of Christianity. The Bible should be in every Christian home. Every aspect of Christian life and worship should reflect in some way what God says to his people. Catholics have not always been very good at reading and studying the Bible. In 1965 during the Second Vatican Council a document on Scripture as the Word of God (*Dei Verbum*) was published. This has had a marked effect in laying the foundations for an official programme of encouragement to Catholics to make the Bible central to their lives.

Much has happened since then. Every public act of worship has its readings from Scripture. Scripture (both Old and New Testaments) has a significant place in all religious education programmes, whether for adults or for children. The lectionary for the readings at daily and Sunday Mass covers a large amount of Scripture during its three-year cycle. Familiar acts of devotion like the Rosary and the Stations of the Cross have become far more scripturally based.

The positive value of this is obvious enough. But it

has also meant that many Catholics have been thrown in at the deep end. They are a little like the Ethiopian in his carriage on the way home from Jerusalem who was reading some Scripture. Philip the Deacon heard him and asked him if he understood what he was reading. 'How can I', the man said, 'unless I have someone to guide me?' (Acts 8:26–40). Most of us do need help if we are to understand what we are reading. It is not that the language of Scripture is particularly difficult; it is rather that its context is so often unfamiliar.

I warmly welcome this series of *Scripture for Living*. Its particular value is that it helps us to see how Scripture is relevant in our daily lives. There are many other books for scholars. This series is for ordinary Christians who treasure Scripture, know for certain that it is of fundamental importance, but who are not sure how to make sense of what they read or how to relate it to their daily lives and experiences.

The pattern of the series is story, bible passage, commentary, reflection and prayer. There is a natural progression in this. The writings in the Bible (which form a whole library really) are about people trying to recognise God in their lives. So the context is just everyday life – the stuff of story. Story leads naturally to Scripture because Scripture is itself about life in all its variety. So it speaks of love and hate, success and failure, death and resurrection; almost every imaginable human failing and strength finds place in it, simply because it is about real people. The commentary is an aid to understanding. Then, since the ultimate purpose of Scripture is to lead people closer to God, the text finishes with a prayer which ties together what has gone before and shows how our daily lives can be enriched.

The series is ideal for use in groups as well as by individuals. I wish it every success.

+ DAVID KONSTANT
Bishop of Leeds

Preface

◆━━━◆

WHAT'S THE POINT OF IT ALL? Any Christian, any human being, is likely to be faced with this question more than once in a lifetime. Life is full of experiences which make us stop and think. Out of our boredom and frustration, out of our hopes and expectations, out of our relationships and our struggles, out of our responsibilities and our failures, out of our achievements and our sins, our of our joys and our anxieties, the question springs up for us: what's the point of it all? Whether I am a growing child or a concerned parent, whether I am an adolescent or an adult in the world today, I am likely to ask the question. Unless I ask it, I cannot grow into mature faith. I suppose that, to some extent, this has always been the case, but the Second Vatican Council noted that for twentieth-century Christians who share the joys, hopes, griefs and anxieties of their fellow men and women, life in the world today raises the question with a special intensity. The question is not theoretical but practical and spiritual: it is addressed to 'humankind, body and soul, heart and conscience, mind and will'.[1] It challenges me to get clearer about my reasons for living and hoping, so I can be ready to share them with others. I meet people constantly who are searching for 'reasons for living and hoping'. The 1965 Constitution which I have just quoted remarks, 'Although the human race today is proud of its achievements and its abilities, it is frequently concerned about modern developments in the world, about humanity's place and role on the planet, about the meaning of individual and corporate endeavours, and about the ultimate purpose of things and human beings'.[2] In other words, it wonders: 'What is the point of it all?'

Although for some Christians, education in faith is all about learning the Church's answers to important questions, most people agree that the questions themselves need first to be owned and pondered – as I have discovered them in my own experience of life. Then the rich body of answers, opened up in the Scriptures and in the lives of Christians, can be appreciated. 'In language intelligible to each generation, (the Church) can respond to the perennial questions which people ask about this present life and the life to come, and about the relationship of the one to the other.'[3]

To Steve, one of my former students and best friends, that I should attempt to write such a book must seem very pretentious. After all, 'What is the point of it all?' is a question to which each person must search for a personal answer. Prepackaged answers will always be inadequate. But Steve will understand when I say that the book is as much about asking the question as about finding an answer to it. I write 'an answer' rather than 'the answer', for I believe there are many answers, that I must sift through other people's answers as I search for my own, and that God will be with me in the sifting and choosing.

This book consists of nine essays. Some contain stories of struggle and hope, some contain stories of resurrection, some stories of conversion. I have tried to use my experience of Christians I have met (either in real life or in their writings) who have helped me to see how Scripture raises the question 'What's the point of it all?' and who supply answers to that question. In each chapter, the reader is invited to enter imaginatively into the story and to reflect prayerfully on the questions and answers it offers. The people I have written about are people who continue to speak powerfully to me today. As the author of Hebrews writes of Abel, when praising him with other ancestors for his exemplary faith, 'Though he is dead, he still speaks by faith' (Hebrews 11:4). The life and example of everyone mentioned in this book has offered me inspiration and encouragement. Through them, as through the Scriptures, God continues to speak to me and to call me. 'What is the point of it all?' is a question which compels believers to listen reflectively to what God might be saying and also to respond to what we hear.

A few parts of this book use material previously published in short articles by the author, or used in talks in recent years. All the introductory stories are true, but in some of them the names of characters have been changed.

Steve, old friend and fellow-searcher, this book is for you. And it is also for Jim, Anne and Bernadette with whom I work. All four of you provide me with inspiration and encouragement in different and complementary ways. Thank you.

DAMIAN LUNDY FSC

Job

I FIRST MET DONALD fourteen years ago, when he was seventeen. He came with a group of sixth-formers from a town in the north of England to make a week-end retreat at St Cassian's Centre in Kintbury, Berkshire, where I was working. During an introductory session, we were all invited to share something of our background. Donald explained that he had been born in Northern Ireland. His father, suffering from a serious heart ailment, had been advised by his doctor to cross the Irish Sea to move to a less stressful part of Britain. The family had talked the matter over and agreed to follow the doctor's advice. They moved to Merseyside, where, a few days later, physically and emotionally disturbed by the sheer effort involved in the change, Donald's father had a heart attack and died.

Three days later, leaving nine year-old Donald with a neighbour, his mother and teenage sister drove to the airport to meet relatives who were flying over for the funeral. In the course of their short journey, they had an accident. They collided with another car. Both women were killed instantly. Within three days, Donald was cruelly orphaned – deprived of his three closest relatives.

Moved by Donald's story and by the calm, quiet way in which he told it, I reacted with three questions. How can a person who has suffered so tragically speak so calmly about his experiences and be apparently untouched by anger or bitterness? What brings a person like that to make a weekend retreat? (If God had treated me so cruelly, I do not think I would have been attracted to spend a weekend in prayer and reflection.) Had Donald ever heard of or read the book of Job?

He did not answer the first question directly, though he implied an answer in his response to the second one. He described how he had been adopted by a wonderful family whose faith, hope and love had been a continuing healing experience in his life. The circle of Christian friends among whom he lived had offered him love and acceptance. As a normal adolescent he had the same problems as everyone else. He had come with his friends to make a weekend retreat in the hope that he would find further help and inspiration. No, he did not know the book of Job, though he knew there was such a book in the Bible.

◆━━━━◆

> How deserted she sits,
>   the city once thronged with people!
> Once the greatest of nations,
>   she is now like a widow.
> Once the princess of states,
>   she is now put to forced labour.
>
> All night long she is weeping,
>   tears running down her cheeks.
> Not one of all her lovers
>   remains to comfort her.

*Her friends have all betrayed her
and become her enemies.*

*Judah has gone into exile
after much pain and toil.
Living among the nations
she finds no respite;
her persecutors all overtake her
where there is no way out.*
(Lamentations 1, 1–3)

*Perish the day on which I was born
and the night that told of a boy conceived.
May that day be darkness,
may God on high have no thought for it,
may no light shine on it.*

*Why was I not still-born,
or why did I not perish as I left the womb?
Why were there knees to receive me,
breasts for me to suck?*
(Job: 3:3–4, 11–12)

If you have read the book of Job, you will realise why Donald's story reminded me of Job's. We don't know when Job was written but it was almost certainly after the Jews returned from exile in Babylon in 538 BC. Solomon's magnificent temple, the centre of the Jewish cult, was destroyed after the siege and capture of Jerusalem in 587. The awful desolation is described in Lamentations which is thought to have been written by the prophet Jeremiah. A series of deportations to Babylon followed the capture of Jerusalem. The captivity and exile brought about a great crisis of faith for the Jewish people, but the experience of suffering was responsible for a remarkable maturing of faith – as has frequently been found to happen when people have been forced to face the painful question, 'What's the point of it all?' After the return from exile, the Temple was rebuilt in 520.

Many critics have felt that in its preoccupation with unbearable suffering, the book of Job is a meditation on a search for the meaning of life in the face of unbearable grief. The author takes the old legend of the patriarchal figure of Job, famed for his patience, and uses it to reflect on the complexity of the relationship between God and humankind. It is an attempt, through poetry, to make sense of God's justice, when God appears to treat harshly and unjustly a man whose life has been spent in God-fearing righteousness and faithful service. Job is a passionately written literary masterpiece: passages of intensely dramatic verse are set within the retelling of an old legend. Job, 'a sound and honest man who feared God and shunned evil' (Job 1:11) is afflicted by God at Satan's request with the loss of all his possessions and his children, and with a painful and humiliating illness. He refuses to curse God despite the attitude of his wife who confronts him: 'Why persist in this integrity of yours? Curse God and die.' Job's reaction to the loss of his ten children and his animals had been to say:

> Naked I came from my mother's womb,
> naked I shall return again.
> Yahweh gave, Yahweh has taken back.
> Blessed be the name of Yahweh!
> (Job 1:21)

The writer adds, 'In all this misfortune Job committed no sin, and he did not reproach God.' (v. 22)

Three of his friends, Eliphaz, Bildad and Zophar, come to visit Job in his grief, 'to offer him sympathy and consolation' (Job 2:12) but in reality adding to his depression. After seven days and nights of silence, Job gives way and curses the day of his birth. He and his friends now take part in a great debate about life in relation to God, which forms the central core of the book. In powerful verse, Job pours out his feelings:

> My only food is sighs,
>> and my groans pour out like water.
> Whatever I fear comes true,
>> whatever I dread befalls me.
> For me, there is no calm, no peace;
>> my torments banish rest.
>
> (Job 3:24–6)

His three 'comforters' insist that 'blessed are those whom God corrects' (Job 5:17), Job is not satisfied and wrestles with the injustice of undeserved suffering for he has 'never rebelled against the Holy One's decrees'. (Job 6:10) How can anyone claim to be upright before a God who 'moves the mountains, though they do not know it; he throws them down when he is angry.' (Job 9:5). He ponders the apparent hopelesness of human life, 'fleeting as a shadow' (Job 14:2), and despairs.

Eventually, 'from the heart of the tempest', God gives Job his answer:

> Who is this, obscuring my intentions
>> with his ignorant words?
> Brace yourself like a fighter;

> I am going to ask the questions, and you are to
>   inform me!
> Where were you when I laid the earth's
>   foundations?
>   Tell me, since you are so well-informed!
> Who decided its dimensions, do you know?
>   Or who stretched the measuring line across it?
>
> (Job 38:2–5)

Job's response to God is to acknowledge the unbridge-
able gulf between God's mysteriousness and human
ignorance:

> I was the man who misrepresented your intentions
>   with my ignorant words.
> You have told me about great works that I cannot
>   understand,
>   about marvels which are beyond me, of which I
>   know nothing.
> Before, I knew you only by hearsay
>   but now, having seen you with my own eyes,
> I retract what I have said,
>   and repent in dust and ashes.
>
> (Job 42:3, 5–6)

God acknowledges Job's irreproachable goodness and
blesses his latter condition even more than his former
one – with rich possessions, a large and beautiful
family and a long life. This 'happy ending' is hardly
convincing for modern readers. The mystery of God's
ways remains: there is no way in which God can be
explained or understood. The editor of the New Jerusalem Bible comments:

> This is the book's lesson: faith must remain even

when understanding fails. At this stage of divine revelation, the author could go no further. More light cannot be thrown on the mystery of suffering innocence until God opens up the prospect of a future life in which recompense is made and reveals the worth of suffering when it is united with the suffering of Christ.[4]

He then adds that 'two texts of Paul give Job his answer', but we must leave Paul until the next chapter.

FOR PRAYER AND REFLECTION

1. Reflect on your life and divide the sufferings you have experienced into two categories: 'deserved' and 'undeserved'. What has suffering taught you about yourself? What has suffering taught you about your God?
2. Have you ever met anyone who has suffered as terribly as Donald or Job? Have you ever met anyone embittered or poisoned by suffering? What impressed or depressed you about these people?
3. What is the most profound novel, poem, music or work of art you have discovered which reflects on the nature of suffering? What have you learned from it?
4. Using the inspiration which the Book of Job may supply, write your own poem or prayer about a loss or bereavement which you have suffered, or pray Psalm 103 slowly, pausing after each line.

Paul: A Letter to the
Philippians

❖

SIMON WAS A SIXTEEN YEAR-OLD lad from South
Wales who came to our retreat centre in the summer
of 1984. We always emphasised the importance of helping young people to appreciate and accept themselves
as individuals, as well as to seek to grow together in
faith, hope and love. In this context, our Eucharists
were, as you might expect, occasions of real cele-
bration, and we encouraged everyone to make a
personal contribution through participation in music,
ritual and prayer. One part of the liturgy which usually
assumed special importance was the sign of peace. One
reason why I remember Simon was that he spent the
entire ten minutes or so exchanging a prolonged sign
of peace, an extended passionate hug, with a girl he
had met at the centre. I had to intervene, and later to
explain the point of the sign of peace within a Eucharist. He accepted the mild rebuke very graciously and
referred to it as a learning-experience in a letter he
wrote to me some weeks later.

In the same letter he described how, with his friends,
he had approached his parish priest to organise a youth-
liturgy in the parish. He was surprised by the priest's

willingness to respond – even to the extent of buying a new set of hymnals. The experience helped to revitalise the younger end of the parish.

Simon's retreat awakened in him a real hunger for God. 'Taste and see that the Lord is good.' He had tasted and he had seen. He took to reading Scripture and to setting aside time for personal prayer. He discovered Thomas à Kempis' *Imitation of Christ* and read this medieval work of devotion with enthusiasm and curiosity. He had entered upon a conversion experience. He even started to write hymns.

Above all he reflected very critically about himself and his relationships, especially his relationship with his seventeen-year-old spastic sister. She was in a wheelchair and had little control over her muscles. Until now he had experienced only embarrassment in her regard, now he forgot the embarrassment and turned to Mary in love. He took her for walks, and prayed and thought about her unceasingly. Her presence in his life helped him to find God. This is what he said about Mary in his letter:

> Another thing that I have done is to take my spastic sister, Mary, for a walk in the wheelchair. You know, Damian, up until the week in Kintbury, I had never taken her for a walk. Now I have taken her for five walks. It's not much but it doesn't half make her happy – and seeing Mary happy makes me happy. There are difficult times though, and she cries a lot because she gets frustrated and realises that I can go out and walk and talk, and she can't. She usually cries due to my impatience, unkindness, selfishness, lack of understanding, etc. I just can't understand why some people suffer and others don't. But I tell you, Damian, my

family would not be complete without her presence. I honestly believe that she must be blessed in some way or another. She's so helpful to me and the rest of the family in the sense that we realise how fortunate we are to be able to walk, talk, write, read and lots more. I really thank God for that sister of mine and I really love her a lot. I usually get very emotional when I talk about her to other people. The more I talk and write about my sister, the more I grow to love her and find out what a special and very interesting girl she is.

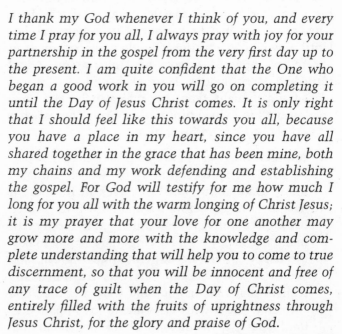

I thank my God whenever I think of you, and every time I pray for you all, I always pray with joy for your partnership in the gospel from the very first day up to the present. I am quite confident that the One who began a good work in you will go on completing it until the Day of Jesus Christ comes. It is only right that I should feel like this towards you all, because you have a place in my heart, since you have all shared together in the grace that has been mine, both my chains and my work defending and establishing the gospel. For God will testify for me how much I long for you all with the warm longing of Christ Jesus; it is my prayer that your love for one another may grow more and more with the knowledge and complete understanding that will help you to come to true discernment, so that you will be innocent and free of any trace of guilt when the Day of Christ comes, entirely filled with the fruits of uprightness through Jesus Christ, for the glory and praise of God.

(Philippians 1:3–11)

When God comes into your life, you start to change. All your relationships are affected. Your eyes are opened to the amazing grace of God's presence. What happened to Simon has happened to many. It happened to Saul of Tarsus, turning him into the greatest Christian missionary, a man of passionate and untiring zeal.

One of Paul's shorter and most easily understood letters is the one to the Christian community at Philippi in Macedonia. Here Paul had begun his mission to Europe in AD 50. Acts 16 describes how Paul at Troas in Asia (modern Turkey) had a vision: 'A Macedonian appeared and kept urging him in these words, "Come across to Macedonia and help us." Once he had seen this vision we lost no time in arranging a passage to Macedonia, convinced that God had called us to bring them the good news. Sailing from Troas we made a straight run for Samothrace; the next day for Neapolis, and from there for Philippi, a Roman colony and the principal city of that district of Macedonia' (Acts 16:9–12).

The rest of Acts 16 describes how Paul's work of evangelisation in the city led to his meeting an impressive business-woman named Lydia, who responded to Paul's message and who insisted that he make her home his base. 'And she would take no refusal' (v. 15). This stay in Philippi included a spell in prison, a flogging, an earthquake and the subsequent conversion of the jailor and his family. It is obvious that, for Paul, Philippi was a place he would not easily forget.

The idealised account in Acts was written over twenty years after Paul's letter to the Philippians. Scholars used to believe that this letter was written from prison in Rome not long before Paul's martyrdom there in AD 67. It is clear from the letter that Paul wrote it from prison, but most scholars now believe that it was

written from a prison in Ephesus in AD 56–57. In 2
Corinthians, Paul writes of the hardships he endured
in Ephesus at this time:

> In the hardships we underwent in Asia, we want
> you to be quite certain, brothers, that we were
> under extraordinary pressure, beyond our powers
> of endurance, so that we gave up all hope even of
> surviving. In fact we were carrying the sentence
> of death within our own selves, so that we should
> be forced to trust not in ourselves but in God, who
> raises the dead. He did save us from such a death
> and will save us – we are relying on him to do
> so.
>
> (2 Corinthians 1:8–10)

Although it was written from prison while Paul was
under sentence of death, Philippians is Paul's most
joyful letter. It reflects his real affection for the Christian community in Philippi and thanks them for their
constant support for his work through prayer and gifts
of money. The letter also expresses Paul's concern for
the unity of the community. What he has heard about
disagreements between leading women of the community like Euodia and Synteche (Philippians 4:2)
leads him to propose Christ Jesus as a model of
humility and service for all who profess faith in him.
In the great christological hymn which Paul quotes in
chapter 2, Jesus is contrasted with Adam, made in the
image of God (Genesis 1:27) who, misled by the ser-
pent, tries to make himself equal with God, knowing
good from evil. Crucified like a slave, Jesus 'was hum-
bler yet, even to accepting death, death on a cross'
(Philippians 2:8) 'and for this, God raised him high'
(v. 9) and glorified him to be acknowledged by every
tongue as Lord of the universe.

To believe that Jesus is Lord is no mere pious formula for devotional use in a hymn or a prayer. For Paul, the answer to the question 'What is the point of it all?' came with his discovery and extraordinary experience of Christ Jesus. From his relationship with Christ, Paul's way of thinking changes radically so that the only way in which he can make sense of his life is to see everything that happens to him as happening 'in Christ'. This explains the secret of Paul's overwhelming joy and peace – the joy and peace which he wants his friends at Philippi to experience despite all their tensions and trials; for as Paul wrote in another letter, 'God is a God not of disorder but of peace' (1 Corinthians 14:25).

FOR PRAYER AND REFLECTION

1. Reflect on two or three periods of your life when you have been searching and when you have found peace. Who or what brought you peace?
2. Have you ever met anyone like Simon or Paul whose life was changed by a conversion experience – who experienced a complete transformation of vision, who 'saw the light'? What impressed or astonished you about this person?
3. Reflect on the hymn 'Amazing Grace' by John Newton (1725–1807). Newton, a reckless sailor, flogged as a deserter from the navy and eventually a commander of a slave ship, experienced a conversion to Christianity, partly through reading Thomas à Kempis' *Imitation of Christ* (the book discovered by Simon after his Kintbury experience), and steering a water-logged vessel in danger of death. Later he became a zealous pastor and a leading figure in

the English evangelical revival, and he often reflected on his personal experience in his hymns.

Amazing grace! How sweet the sound
that saved a wretch like me.
I once was lost, but now I'm found,
was blind, but now I see.

'Twas grace that taught my heart to fear,
and grace my fears relieved.
How precious did that grace appear
the hour I first believed.

Through many dangers, toils and snares
I have already come.
'Tis grace hath brought me safe thus far,
and grace will lead me home.

The Lord has promised good to me;
his word my hope secures.
He will my shield and portion be
as long as life endures.

4. A note in the New Jerusalem Bible reflects on two texts of Paul and sees them as the Christian answer to the questions raised by Job.

In my estimation, all that we suffer in the present time is nothing in comparison with the glory which is destined to be disclosed for us, for the whole creation is waiting with eagerness for the children of God to be revealed.

(Romans 8:18–19)

It makes me happy to be suffering for you now,

and in my own body to make up all the hardships that still have to be undergone by Christ for the sake of his body, the Church.

(Colossians 1:24)

What do you think of these texts? In prayer, apply them to your experience.

A Man Born Blind:

John 9

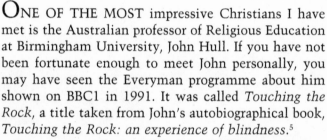

ONE OF THE MOST impressive Christians I have met is the Australian professor of Religious Education at Birmingham University, John Hull. If you have not been fortunate enough to meet John personally, you may have seen the Everyman programme about him shown on BBC1 in 1991. It was called *Touching the Rock*, a title taken from John's autobiographical book, *Touching the Rock: an experience of blindness.*[5]

Born in Victoria in 1935, John Hull gradually lost his sight and became totally blind in 1983, four years after he had remarried. Since June 1983, he has recorded on cassette diary accounts of his daily experiences and feelings. As well as offering a moving personal account of the changes introduced into his life by his blindness, John Hull reflects critically, from his personal experience, on the use of the themes of blindness and light in Scripture.

> One of the most beautiful biblical passages which expresses the power of the archetype of light is found in Numbers 6:24–6, the Aaronic Blessing: 'The Lord bless you and keep you, the Lord make

his face to shine upon you and be gracious unto you, the Lord lift up the light of his countenance upon you and give you peace.' This passage expresses the clarity, the radiance and the sense of identity which is conferred by being in the presence of the lighted face of God.[6]

He reflects on Psalm 139 finding its images particularly appropriate to a blind person:

'I praise thee, for thou art fearful and wonderful. Wonderful are thy works . . . how precious to me are thy thoughts, O God! How vast is the sum of them! If I were to count them, they are more than the sand . . .' [Psalm 139:14ff.].

As a blind person, sitting on the beach, I have poured a fistful of sand upon the palm of my other hand, allowing it to trickle through my fingers. I have rubbed the sand between my finger and thumb, wondering at the various textures. Some of the grains are coarse and sharp, filing the skin in such a way that every little speck stands out. Some are so smooth and silky that it is almost impossible to tell the grains, the sand disappearing like water. If I stretch my hand out a little further, I can still grasp sand, and so on, further and further. I know that with sight I could tell the sweep of this beach for miles around the bay. This beach is but one of thousands of such beaches, and there are probably thousands of people like me just now, doing what I am doing, running the grains between their fingers and wondering. So are the divine thoughts. My body holds them, one by one, while I myself am held like a grain upon the hand of God.

In adoration I welcome the divine knowledge.

'Search me, O God, and know my heart. Try me, and know my thoughts and see if there be any wicked way in me, and lead me in the way everlasting' [Psalm 139:23–4]. What matters is not that I am blind, but that I am known and that I am led by the hand, and that my life, whether sighted or blind, is full of praise.[7]

* * *

As he went along, he saw a man who had been blind from birth. His disciples asked him, 'Rabbi, who sinned, this man or his parents, that he should have been born blind?' 'Neither he nor his parents sinned,' Jesus answered, 'he was born blind so that the works of God might be revealed in him.

> *'As long as day lasts*
> *we must carry out the work of the one*
> *   who sent me;*
> *the night will soon be here*
> *   when no one can work.*
> *As long as I am in the world*
> *I am the light of the world.'*

Having said this, he spat on the ground, made a paste with the spittle, put this over the eyes of the blind man, and said to him, 'Go and wash in the Pool of Siloam' (the name means 'one who has been sent'). So he went off and washed and came back able to see.

His neighbours and the people who used to see him before (for he was a beggar) said, 'Isn't this the man who used to sit and beg?' Some said, 'Yes, it is the same one.' Others said, 'No, but he looks just like

him.' The man himself said, 'Yes, I am the one.' So
they said to him, 'Then how is it that your eyes were
opened?' He answered, 'The man called Jesus made a
paste, daubed my eyes with it and said to me, "Go off
and wash at Siloam"; so I went, and when I washed I
gained my sight.' They asked, 'Where is he?' He
answered, 'I don't know.'

They brought to the Pharisees the man who had been
blind. It had been a Sabbath day when Jesus made
the paste and opened the man's eyes, so when the
Pharisees asked him how he had gained his sight, he
said, 'He put a paste on my eyes and I washed, and I
can see.' Then some of the Pharisees said, 'That man
cannot be from God: he does not keep the Sabbath.'
Others said, 'How can a sinner produce signs like
this?' And there was division among them. So they
spoke to the blind man again, 'What have you to say
about him yourself, now that he has opened your
eyes?' The man answered, 'He is a prophet.'

However, the Jews would not believe that the man
had been blind without first sending for the parents
of the man who had gained his sight and asking them,
'Is this man really the son of yours who you say was
born blind? If so, how is it that he is now able to see?'
His parents answered, 'We know he is our son and we
know he was born blind, but how he can see, we don't
know, nor who opened his eyes. Ask him. He is old
enough: let him speak for himself.' His parents spoke
like this out of fear of the Jews, who had already
agreed to ban from the synagogue anyone who should
acknowledge Jesus as the Christ. This was why his
parents said, 'He is old enough; ask him.'

So the Jews sent for the man again and said to him, 'Give glory to God! We are satisfied that this man is a sinner.' The man answered, 'Whether he is a sinner I don't know; all I know is that I was blind and now I can see.' They said to him, 'What did he do to you? How did he open your eyes?' He replied, 'I have told you once and you wouldn't listen. Why do you want to hear it all again? Do you want to become his disciples yourselves?' At this they hurled abuse at him, 'It is you who are his disciple, we are disciples of Moses: we know that God spoke to Moses, but as for this man, we don't know where he comes from.' The man replied, 'That is just what is so amazing! You don't know where he comes from and he has opened my eyes! We know that God doesn't listen to sinners, but God does listen to people who are devout and do his will. Ever since the world began it is unheard of for anyone to open the eyes of someone born blind; if this man were not from God, he wouldn't have been able to do anything.' They retorted, 'Are you trying to teach us, and you a sinner through and through ever since you were born!' And they ejected him.

Jesus heard they had ejected him, and when he found him he said to him, 'Do you believe in the Son of man?' 'Sir,' the man replied, 'tell me who he is so that I may believe in him.' Jesus said, 'You have seen him; he is speaking to you.' The man said, 'Lord, I believe,' and worshipped him.

Jesus said:

> *It is for judgement*
> *that I have come into this world,*
> *so that those without sight may see*
> *and those with sight may become blind.*

Hearing this, some Pharisees who were present said to him, 'So we are blind, are we?' Jesus replied:

> *If you were blind,*
> *you would not be guilty,*
> *but since you say, 'We can see,'*
> *your guilt remains.*

(John 9)

St John uses the story of Jesus' cure of a blind man (a young man, I suggest) to reflect on the transformation of a person's life when it is illuminated by faith in Jesus, sent by God to be the light of the world. I have divided the chapter into sections. Each section marks a change of scene, the introduction of a new character or group of characters, the development of the drama which is unfolding. You are invited to read the chapter, ideally with a group of friends speaking the different parts, so you can catch a sense of the drama as it unfolds. You could also emphasise any words like 'blind', 'eyes', 'see', etc., so you can capture the richness of the language used to tell the story. Finally you could note the number of question-marks in the narrative, as well as the implicit questions which fill the text. This will open your eyes to the extraordinary richness of this story. We shall then look at some parts of the text in more detail.

It is interesting that the sight of the blind man causes Jesus' disciples to start asking questions about sin and God. In common with most Jews of their time, they assume that blindness is a punishment for sin – either the blind man's own sins or his parents' sins. In a way, the disciples raise the 'What's the point of it all?' question at the very beginning of the incident.

Jesus challenges their understanding of God: 'he was born blind so that the works of God might be revealed in him.' Jesus' notion of God is not that of a God primarily associated with punishment and condemnation, unlike that of so many religious people.

The Pharisees regard themselves as exemplary and law-abiding religious people. But their notion of God is severely limited and contrasts strikingly with that of Jesus. Look again at the use of language in the passage, especially the legal language, words like 'Sabbath', 'judgement', 'guilty'. Note this language in the episodes in which the Pharisees cross-examine the man who had been cured, sending for witnesses like his neighbours and his parents. They expel the man from the synagogue, having put him under oath (using the formula 'Give glory to God!'). The evangelist makes it clear that it is really Jesus (offstage and out of sight throughout most of the story) who is on trial: to the Pharisees, he is a sinner who does not keep the Sabbath, and who cannot therefore be from God.

At the end of the story, Jesus speaks with great authority, making it clear that it is really the Pharisees themselves who are on trial. He charges them with culpable blindness, pronounces them 'guilty', and explains that he has come into the world for judgement.

The passage contrasts the blindness of the religious leaders with the insight, openness and faith of the blind man who has been cured. The works of God have been performed in him, and he is filled with wonder. The Pharisees, with their limited vision, simply miss the point. God is at work in their midst and they fail to recognise him or to respond to the sign which is so dramatically acted out before them.

The stages by which the cured man grows into deeper, more personal faith are particularly striking.

Jesus has taken the initiative in choosing to heal the blind man and in sending him to wash in the Pool of Siloam. The man goes there, without asking any questions. He doesn't know who or where Jesus is, when the neighbours ask him Jesus is simply 'the man called Jesus' (v. 11). By the end of the first interrogation by the Pharisees, the man can answer, 'He is a prophet.' During the second interrogation, the man, with increased confidence, is convinced that Jesus comes from God (v. 33). When Jesus again takes the initiative of seeking out the cured man and asking him, 'Do you believe in the Son of man?' (v. 35), the man's openness and faith have grown even more. 'Tell me who he is so that I may believe in him' (v. 36). Jesus invites the man to use his newly restored eyes: 'You have seen him; he is speaking to you' (v. 37). Using an ancient profession of faith, the man kneels to worship Jesus: 'Lord, I believe' (v. 38). The progression is very moving.

Another important aspect of this chapter is the use of allusions to the two creation accounts in the book of Genesis. Although the Pharisees are proud to call themselves 'disciples of Moses' (traditionally assumed by Jews at that time to be the author of Genesis), they fail to recognise in Jesus 'the work of God'. The primary work of God is creation: the God who began the work of creation (in Genesis 1) by saying, 'Let there be light', is at work in Jesus, 'the light of the world' (v. 5), who carries out the work of the one who sent him (v. 4). In the second (and older) creation account in Genesis 2, God creates Adam 'from the soil of the ground' (Genesis 2:7), over which the water is flowing. Here Jesus spits on the ground and daubs the man's eyes with mud. The Pharisees are blind to the symbolism, although the cured man constantly repeats the detail of how he was cured (vv. 11, 15).

St John uses the story of the man born blind as a symbol of the 'new creation' through baptism (or washing) of which Paul writes in 2 Corinthians, using similar imagery to that used by John in this chapter:

> For anyone who is in Christ, there is a new creation: the old order is gone and a new being is there to see. It is all God's work; he reconciled us to himself through Christ and he gave us the ministry of reconciliation. I mean, God was in Christ reconciling the world to himself, not holding anyone's faults against them, but entrusting to us the message of reconciliation.
>
> So we are ambassadors for Christ; it is as though God were urging you through us, and in the name of Christ we appeal to you to be reconciled to God. For our sake he made the sinless one a victim for sin, so that in him we might become the uprightness of God.
>
> (2 Corinthians 5:17–21)

In the same letter, Paul writes:

> It is not ourselves that we are proclaiming, but Christ Jesus as the Lord, and ourselves as your servants for Jesus' sake. It is God who said, 'Let light shine out of darkness,' that has shone into our hearts to enlighten them with the knowledge of God's glory, the glory on the face of Christ.
>
> (2 Corinthians 4:5–6)

John's account of the healing of the blind man has been used since early times as a depiction of the new life offered to Christians who are baptised in Christ Jesus. It is one of the key readings for the journey of faith made by those who are preparing for baptism during Lent. When this gospel is read on the Fourth

Sunday of Lent, there is a special preface to underline
its significance:

Father, all-powerful and ever-living God,
we do well always and everywhere to give you thanks
through Jesus Christ our Lord.

He came among us as a man,
to lead mankind from darkness
into the light of faith.

Through Adam's fall we were born as slaves of sin,
but now through baptism in Christ
we are reborn as your adopted children.

Earth unites with heaven
to sing the new song of creation,
as we adore and praise you for ever:

FOR PRAYER AND REFLECTION

1. What do you see in this chapter of St John's Gospel
   of your own journey of faith?
2. What do you see in this story of your own blindness
   to the work of God in the world?
3. How do light, darkness and water speak to you of
   God? Use the passages from John 9 and 2 Corinthians in your prayer to praise God for the gifts you
   have received.
4. Like John Hull, pray Psalm 139 meditatively. Like
   him, do you think it might have been written by a
   blind person?

To Live in the Light of the Resurrection:

Reflections on John 20 and 21

IN MEMORABLE WORDS, the bishops of Vatican II spoke of the 'future of humanity' lying 'in the hands of those who are strong enough to provide coming generations with reasons for living and hoping'.[8] That is surely the task of all Christians in the world today, for our Church is called to be an evangelising Church.

I was born in March 1944, and I take particular interest in reading reflections written at that time. They tell me something about the world into which I was born – at a time when the world was at war, when many people were asking 'What's the point of it all?' One of the most reflective of these people was Dietrich Bonhoeffer, the German pastor and theologian. Born in February 1906, he studied at Berlin University and worked in various parts of Europe, including London. The Gestapo forbade him to lecture, write or make speeches. With his brother-in-law, Bonhoeffer became involved in plans to overthrow the Nazi government. He was arrested in April 1943 and spent months reflecting on the meaning of what was happening in the world around him. A brave and sensitive man, he wrote a series of remarkable letters to his family and friends. Several of these letters survive and have been published. Payne Best, an English officer whom Bonhoeffer met in prison, wrote of Bonhoeffer that 'he always seemed to me to diffuse an atmosphere of happiness, of joy in every smallest event in life, and of deep gratitude for the mere fact that he was alive . . . He was one of the very few men that I have ever met to whom his God was real and close'.[9] Bonhoeffer was executed at Flossenburg on 9 April 1945.

On 27 March 1944, Bonhoeffer wrote to a friend, 'We need . . . the resurrection of Christ to invigorate and cleanse the world today . . . What a tremendous difference it would make if a few people really believed and acted upon that. To live in the light of the resurrection – that is the meaning of Easter. Do you not find that so few people seem to know what they live by?'

An underlying reflection of this book is that it is good for us to ask ourselves 'What am I living by?' To link the values of the faith we profess in our worship with our everyday lives is a constant challenge for all Christians. So what might it mean for us to live in the light of the resurrection of Jesus? How does that central mystery of our faith provide us with reasons for living and hoping?

Answers to these questions are offered in the four wonderful stories which make up the last two chapters of St John's Gospel. These stories are read in church on the early Sundays after Easter. I propose to examine these familiar passages and to show how we can use them as mirrors in which to look at reflections of ourselves. Fundamental to each story is the surprise meeting of the risen Jesus with an individual or group of his followers. Or should I say ex-followers?

◆════➤

*It was very early on the first day of the week and still
dark, when Mary of Magdala came to the tomb. She
saw that the stone had been moved away from the
tomb and came running to Simon Peter and the other
disciple, the one whom Jesus loved. 'They have taken
the Lord out of the tomb,' she said, 'and we don't
know where they have put him.'*

*Mary was standing outside near the tomb, weeping.
Then, as she wept, she stooped to look inside, and
saw two angels in white sitting where the body of
Jesus had been, one at the head, the other at the feet.
They said, 'Woman, why are you weeping?' 'They have
taken my Lord away,' she replied, 'and I don't know
where they have put him.' As she said this she turned
round and saw Jesus standing there, though she did
not realise that it was Jesus. Jesus said to her, 'Woman,
why are you weeping? Who are you looking for?' Sup-
posing him to be the gardener, she said, 'Sir, if you
have taken him away, tell me where you have put
him, and I will go and remove him.' Jesus said, 'Mary!'
She turned round then and said to him in Hebrew,
'Rabbuni!' – which means Master. Jesus said to her,
'Do not cling to me, because I have not yet ascended
to the Father. But go to the brothers, and tell them: I
am ascending to my Father and your Father, to my
God and your God.' So Mary of Magdala told the
disciples, 'I have seen the Lord,' and that he had said
these things to her.*

(John 20:1–18)

◆════➤

Before dawn, Mary of Magdala came to the garden
tomb and discovered that it was empty. There was no

sign of Jesus' corpse. In tears, Mary stopped to look inside and answered the question of the two strangers – 'Why are you weeping?' – with the statement, 'They have taken my Lord away, and I do not know where they have put him.' When 'she turned round and saw Jesus standing there', she did not recognise him, even when he asked her 'Why are you weeping? Who are you looking for?'

Why did she not know Jesus? Because she was blinded by grief. She was looking for a missing corpse, not for the living Jesus. She must have turned back to the tomb, for when Jesus called her by her name, 'Mary', we are told she turned round and called him 'Rabbuni' before clinging to him in a rapture of joy.

The picture reminds us of the impassioned bride in chapter 3 of the Song of Songs, searching everywhere for her beloved and, having found him, wanting to hold him and not let him go. This passage is used as the first reading in the Mass for the memorial of St Mary Magdalene on 22 July.

Jesus tells Mary not to cling to him, he sends her to his brothers with a message about God: 'I am ascending to my Father and your Father, to my God and your God.' The implication is that the God who has done this for me will do equally wonderful things for you: he is your God as well as mine.

FOR PRAYER AND REFLECTION

1. 'Blessed are those who mourn: they shall be comforted' (Matthew 5:5). How can grief become an occasion for the living God to meet us and transform us? Do you know anyone who has experienced this?

2. The weeping Mary is a symbol of all those who

grieve because they have experienced that Jesus has died and they are missing him. Has there ever been a time when you could identify with her?

3. Mary's turning to Jesus in rapturous joy is a model of conversion for all who mourn, for all whom the Lord surprises in their grief when he calls them tenderly by name. If your life has been full of grieving, Mary is a model for you. May you turn to the Lord and know his peace.

4. What message is the risen Jesus entrusting to you to share with his brothers and sisters? How will you share the good news?

5. You are invited to pray the collect for St Mary Magdalene's Day:

Father,
your Son first entrusted to St Mary Magdalene
the joyful news of his resurrection.
By her prayers and example
may we proclaim Christ as our living Lord
and one day see him in glory

In the evening of that same day, the first day of the week, the doors were closed in the room where the disciples were, for fear of the Jews. Jesus came and stood among them. He said to them, 'Peace be with you,' and, after saying this, he showed them his hands and his side. The disciples were filled with joy at seeing the Lord, and he said to them again, 'Peace be with you.

> *As the Father sent me,
> so am I sending you.'*

After saying this he breathed on them and said:

Receive the Holy Spirit.
If you forgive anyone's sins,
they are forgiven;
if you retain anyone's sins,
they are retained.
(John 20:19–23)

Closed doors are the visual symbol of the second story. The disciples were imprisoned in their fear. Jesus came and stood among them, twice saying 'Peace be with you'.

Peace is the opposite of fear. If you are afraid, you have no inner peace. But seeing Jesus, alive and in their midst, marked with wounds which are now a sign of victory rather than pain and humiliation, the disciples are filled with joy. Peace and joy replace their fear, but these gifts of the Spirit (Galatians 5: 22) are not just for themselves.

Jesus sends out his disciples. He entrusts them with an apostolic mission, his mission: 'As the Father sent me, so am I sending you.' Then he breathes on them and says, 'Receive the Holy Spirit.' In John's Gospel, this is when Pentecost occurs: the risen and crucified Lord, who 'gave up his spirit' on the cross (John 19:30), now breathes it into his disciples. Empowered with the life of God, their mission will be to go out and forgive sins. If they remain locked up in their fears, others will remain 'retained' in their sins, locked up and imprisoned.

Jesus promises, 'If you forgive anyone's sins, they are forgiven.' He adds, by implication, 'if you retain anyone's sins (by not going out and forgiving them) they are retained'. The power to forgive is an Easter gift of the risen Christ, entrusted to Christians to share generously in a world where so many are imprisoned in fear and sin. Not to share this gift is to retain people in their sin. Jesus does not want this.

FOR PRAYER AND REFLECTION

1. Imagine yourself in the upper room with the disciples. You are paralysed with fear. The risen Jesus comes into the room and says 'Peace be with you.' How do you react? How do you feel?
2. Keep the image of the wounded Jesus before your eyes as you read slowly and meditatively these words.

   Christ suffered for you
   and left an example for you to follow in his steps.
   He had done nothing wrong, and had spoken no
      deceit.
   He was insulted and did not retaliate with insults;
   when he was suffering he made no threats
   but put his trust in the upright judge.
   He was bearing our sins in his own body on the
      cross,
   so that we might die to our sins and live for
      uprightness;
   through his bruises you have been healed.
   You had gone astray like sheep
   but now you have returned to the shepherd and
      guardian of your souls.

                                        (1 Peter 2:21–25)

3. Who is Jesus asking you to forgive? How will you do so?
4. Which fruit(s) of the Holy Spirit need to be renewed in you? Ask the Lord for the gift of his Spirit.

5. You are invited to pray thoughtfully:

Lord Jesus Christ, you said to your apostles:
I leave you peace, my peace I give you.
Look not on our sins, but on the faith of your
   Church,
and grant us the peace and unity of your kingdom
where you live for ever and ever.

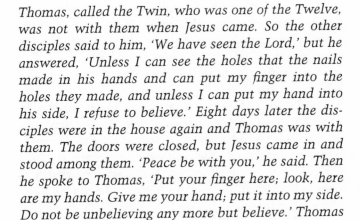

*Thomas, called the Twin, who was one of the Twelve,
was not with them when Jesus came. So the other
disciples said to him, 'We have seen the Lord,' but he
answered, 'Unless I can see the holes that the nails
made in his hands and can put my finger into the
holes they made, and unless I can put my hand into
his side, I refuse to believe.' Eight days later the disciples were in the house again and Thomas was with
them. The doors were closed, but Jesus came in and
stood among them. 'Peace be with you,' he said. Then
he spoke to Thomas, 'Put your finger here; look, here
are my hands. Give me your hand; put it into my side.
Do not be unbelieving any more but believe.' Thomas
replied, 'My Lord and my God!' Jesus said to him:*

*You believe because you can see me.
Blessed are those who have not seen and yet believe.*

*There were many other signs that Jesus worked in the
sight of the disciples, but they are not recorded in this
book. These are recorded so that you may believe that
Jesus is the Christ, the Son of God, and that believing
this you may have life through his name.*

(John 20:24–31)

The first person with whom the disciples want to share the good news is one of their own group, Thomas, who 'was not with them when Jesus came'. Unconvinced by their message, he lays down his conditions for believing: to see and touch Jesus' wounds. Eight days later, Jesus comes to Thomas in his unbelief, again with a greeting of peace. His invitation to Thomas is to touch his wounded hands and side, to cease his doubting and to believe.

Thomas's famous response, 'My Lord and my God' is the classic act of faith and truly the climax of the whole Gospel of John. It is the only time in a Gospel story when Jesus is addressed directly as 'God', but the repeated adjective 'my' points to the intensely personal nature of the faith which Thomas professes, faith which is a gift of Jesus.

The Lord's pronouncement, 'Blessed are those who have not seen and yet believe' leads to the sentence which tells us why the Gospel was written, words which were probably the concluding sentence of John's Gospel in its original edition: 'recorded so that you may believe that Jesus is the Christ, the Son of God, and that believing this you may have life through his name.' Here is a striking statement of Christian 'reasons for living and hoping'. Thomas's refusal to believe has been replaced by a living personal faith in Jesus as his Lord and his God. That is the kind of faith offered to all who hear the gospel and respond to its power to give life. In addressing his readers directly, 'that you may believe', the evangelist is addressing us today: grieving, fearful, doubting, but called by the risen Lord to abundant life (John 10:10), eternal life (John 6:40): 'whoever lives and believes in me will never die' (John 11:25).

FOR PRAYER AND REFLECTION

1. Imagine Jesus saying to you, 'Put your finger here; look, here are my hands. Give me your hand; put it into my side. Do not be unbelieving any more but believe.' How do you respond?
2. Thank God for the gift of faith. Remind yourself of those who have shared faith with you. Thank God for their faith.
3. Have you ever tried to share your faith with unbelievers? Pray for the courage and trust to do this.
4. You are invited to pray thoughtfully:

Almighty Father,
as we honour Thomas the apostle,
let us always experience the help of his prayers.
May we have eternal life by believing in Jesus,
whom Thomas acknowledged as Lord.

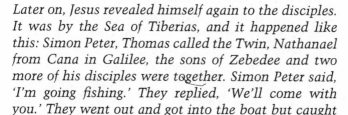

Later on, Jesus revealed himself again to the disciples. It was by the Sea of Tiberias, and it happened like this: Simon Peter, Thomas called the Twin, Nathanael from Cana in Galilee, the sons of Zebedee and two more of his disciples were together. Simon Peter said, 'I'm going fishing.' They replied, 'We'll come with you.' They went out and got into the boat but caught nothing that night.

When it was already light, there stood Jesus on the shore, though the disciples did not realise that it was Jesus. Jesus called, out, 'Haven't you caught anything, friends?' And when they answered, 'No,' he said, 'Throw the net out to starboard and you'll find something.' So they threw the net out and could not haul it in because of the quantity of fish. The disciple

whom Jesus loved said to Peter, 'It is the Lord.' At
these words, 'It is the Lord,' Simon Peter tied his
outer garment round him (for he had nothing on) and
jumped into the water. The other disciples came on
in the boat, towing the net with the fish; they were
only about a hundred yards from land.

As soon as they came ashore they saw that there
was some bread there and a charcoal fire with fish
cooking on it. Jesus said, 'Bring some of the fish you
have just caught.' Simon Peter went aboard and drag-
ged the net ashore, full of big fish, one hundred and
fifty-three of them; and in spite of there being so many
the net was not broken. Jesus said to them, 'Come
and have breakfast.' None of the disciples was bold
enough to ask, 'Who are you?'. They knew quite well
it was the Lord. Jesus then stepped forward, took the
bread and gave it to them, and the same with the fish.
This was the third time that Jesus revealed himself to
the disciples after rising from the dead.

When they had eaten, Jesus said to Simon Peter,
'Simon son of John, do you love me more than these
others do?' He answered, 'Yes, Lord, you know I love
you.' Jesus said to him, 'Feed my lambs.' A second
time he said to him, 'Simon son of John, do you love
me?' He replied, 'Yes, Lord, you know I love you.'
Jesus said to him, 'Look after my sheep.' Then he said
to him a third time, 'Simon son of John, do you love
me?' Peter was hurt that he asked him a third time,
'Do you love me?' and said, 'Lord, you know everything; you know I love you.' Jesus said to him, 'Feed
my sheep.

> In all truth I tell you,
> when you were young
> you put on your own belt

> *and walked where you liked;*
> *but when you grow old*
> *you will stretch out your hands,*
> *and somebody else*
>   *will put a belt round you*
> *and take you*
>   *where you would rather not go.'*

In these words he indicated the kind of death by which Peter would give glory to God. After this he said, 'Follow me.'

(John 21:1–19)

❧

Chapter 21 of John's Gospel is an epilogue, perhaps written by the evangelist in a second edition of his book, perhaps added early by a disciple of the evangelist. It is a beautifully told story of a meeting between the risen Jesus and Simon Peter on the shore of Lake Tiberias in Galilee.

To his six companions, Peter has announced, 'I'm going fishing'. It has been suggested that these words point to a return to the way life was before Jesus disturbed it. Peter is an ex-disciple, a failure, but he is a born leader, and the others say, 'We'll come with you'. As in Luke 5:5, Peter is not a good fisherman, and catches nothing all night until Jesus stands at the water's edge 'when it was already light'.

At the stranger's word, the fishermen catch one hundred and fifty-three big fish – seen by many commentators as a symbol of the catholicity of the Church: it is for everyone. Then – a delightful touch – the Lord invites the disciples to 'come and have breakfast'. The meal is described in eucharistic terms: 'Jesus . . . took the bread and gave it to them, and the same with the fish'.

Eucharist is followed by reconciliation. The first thing Peter saw as he came ashore was 'some bread there and a charcoal fire with some fish cooking on it'. The charcoal fire could not have failed to remind him of his threefold denial of Jesus, since this had taken place outside the door of the high priest's palace where 'the servants and guards had lit a charcoal fire and were warming themselves; so Peter stood there too, warming himself with the others' (John 18:18). It was here that, when asked three times if he were not one of Jesus' disciples, he denied it three times before the cock crew – as Jesus had predicted (John 13:38).

A new start is needed, and after breakfast, Jesus asks Simon Peter, 'Do you love me?' It is an emotional question, asked three times, and it is therefore an opportunity to move beyond the threefold denial to a fresh start. Understandably Peter feels moved. Who wouldn't be?

The fact that Jesus addresses his old follower as 'Simon son of John' each time is also to be noted, for John tells us that the Lord's very first words to the man he was to choose to lead his community had been, 'You are Simon son of John; you are to be called Cephas', which means Peter or rock (John 1:42). Now we see Jesus taking Peter back to the start of their relationship, and giving him another chance, another call.

Peter's vocation will involve a change of job, from fisherman to shepherd: 'Feed my lambs . . . Look after my sheep . . . Feed my sheep.' In John 10, Jesus described the characteristics of the good shepherd – in contrast with the hired man, 'the good shepherd lays down his life for his sheep' (John 10:11). Peter is asked to take care of Jesus' flock, not his own. And now Jesus predicts the martyr's death 'by which Peter would give glory to God', just as Jesus' death had done (John 17:1), since the converted Peter would prove to be a faithful follower of Jesus and a good shepherd of his flock. The Lord then renews Peter's call to discipleship by saying, 'Follow me.'

FOR PRAYER AND REFLECTION

1. Try to enter into the story of Jesus' meeting with Peter on the shore of Tiberias, by imagining that Jesus comes to meet you when you feel that you have denied him or excluded him from your life. The charcoal fire was an appropriate image for Peter. What is an appropriate image for you?

   Jesus asked Peter, 'Simon, son of John, do you love me?' What does he ask you? Hear him addressing you by name and respond to him.
2. Jesus renews his invitation to you to be a disciple. He says, 'Follow me.' How do you respond? How do you feel? What is your prayer?
3. 'When you were young . . . but when you grow old . . .' What has become clearer to you about God in the course of your life? Are there any questions which still trouble you? How will you deal with them?
4. Do you agree that, given his human weaknesses, St Peter is an appropriate leader for a church of sinners? Do you see in the story of Jesus and Peter any reasons for living and hoping?
5. You are invited to pray the collect for the Solemnity of Saints Peter and Paul.

Praise to you, the God and Father of our Lord Jesus
    Christ,
who in your great mercy
have given us new birth and hope
through the power of Christ's resurrection.
Through the prayers of the apostles Peter and Paul
may we who received this faith through their
    preaching
share their joy in following the Lord
to the unfading inheritance
reserved for us in heaven.

Francis of Assisi

ONE OF THE MOST intriguing saints of the Middle Ages, Francis was born in Assisi in 1182. He was the son of a wealthy cloth merchant, Pietro di Bernardone, who had married a French noblewoman. Francis was a leader of Assisi's young people and rode with the local army to fight against the nearby city of Perugia in 1202. He was captured and imprisoned. An illness led him to examine his life closely: several experiences in 1205 and 1206 led to his conversion. As you will appreciate from this short essay, it is impossible to separate the facts from the legends. Nor do I think that would be desirable.

An act of generosity towards a poor knight with whom Francis exchanged clothes was followed by a vision of a palace where a beautiful lady was awaiting him. He was to realise eventually that she was the Lady Poverty. When he was at Spoleto, on his way to join the papal army, Francis heard a voice in the night which asked him what he was planning to do. When he said he was on his way to join the pope's army, the voice asked him, 'Who is more important, the servant or the master?' He answered, 'The master,' and was told, 'Why then do you seek the servant instead of the master? Go home, for what I have shown you in the

vision of the palace will be fulfilled in you by me –
but in a spiritual way.' Francis started to spend more
time with God, in prayer.

Francis abhorred the sight of lepers. There is a story
that one day he overcame his feelings and embraced a
leper. In the astonished leper's eyes he saw Christ.
Shortly before his death in 1226, Francis dictated this
to Brother Leo:

> This is how the Lord gave me, Brother Francis, the
> grace to begin to do penance: when I was yet in
> my sins, it seemed to me unbearably bitter to see
> lepers. And the Lord himself led me among them,
> and I showed kindness towards them. And as I
> went away from them, that which had seemed
> bitter to me was now changed for me into sweet-
> ness of mind and body. And then I tarried yet a
> little while, and left the world.[10]

The most moving of all the stories from this part of
Francis' life is what happened in the ruined church of
San Damiano where the young man was praying before
the crucifix now venerated in the Basilica of Saint
Clare in Assisi. He prayed, 'Lord, what do you want
me to do?' The figure on the cross told him, 'Francis,
repair my house which, as you see, is falling into
ruins.' He understood Jesus' words literally and started
to rebuild the ruined church. Later, he would understand that the church he was being asked to rebuild
was a church of living stones. I Peter 2: 4, describes
Jesus as 'the living stone, rejected by human beings
but chosen by God and precious to him'. We are told
that Francis could never again think of or speak of a
crucifix without bursting into tears.

Francis' strange behaviour led to increased tension
at home, especially with his father. He started selling

his father's expensive cloth to buy stone to rebuild ruined churches; he started to give expensive cloth to the poor. Pietro denounced his son in front of the local bishop. In public, before the bishop's palace, Francis removed all his clothes, gave them back to his father and said, 'Until today I have called you, Pietro Bernadone, my father on earth. From now on I can surely say "Our Father who art in heaven", for in him I place all my treasure, and all my faith and hope.' Francis now spent his time helping the poor and the sick, and repairing various ruined churches in the area round Assisi.

He summoned his twelve disciples and gave them authority over unclean spirits with power to drive them out and to cure all kinds of disease and all kinds of illness.

These are the names of the twelve apostles: first, Simon who is known as Peter, and his brother Andrew; James the son of Zebedee, and his brother John; Philip and Bartholomew; Thomas, and Matthew the tax collector; James the son of Alphaeus, and Thaddaeus; Simon the Zealot and Judas Iscariot, who was also his betrayer. These twelve Jesus sent out, instructing them as follows:

'Do not make your way to gentile territory, and do not enter any Samaritan town; go instead to the lost sheep of the House of Israel. And as you go, proclaim that the kingdom of Heaven is close at hand. Cure the sick, raise the dead, cleanse those suffering from virulent skin-diseases, drive out devils. You received without charge, give without charge. Provide yourselves with no gold or silver, not even with coppers for your purses, with no haversack for the journey or

spare tunic or footware or a staff, for the labourer
deserves his keep.

'Whatever town or village you go into, seek out
someone worthy and stay with him until you leave.
As you enter his house, salute it, and if the house
deserves it, may your peace come upon it; if it does
not, may your peace come back to you. And if anyone
does not welcome you or listen to what you have to
say, as you walk out of the house or town shake the
dust from your feet. In truth I tell you, on the Day of
Judgement it will be more bearable for Sodom and
Gomorrah than for that town. Look, I am sending you
out like sheep among wolves; so be cunning as snakes
and yet innocent as doves.'

(Matthew 10:1–16)

On 24 February 1209, the feast of St Matthew, Francis
heard this passage read in church, and was moved to
understand it literally. Dressed in a simple tunic, he
became a wandering preacher, sharing a message of
love and peace. Other young men were moved by his
words. They joined him as his disciples and became a
community of brothers. Francis drew up a rule of life
for them, based on the Gospels. In 1210, Pope Innocent
III, who had seen Francis in a dream supporting Rome's
cathedral church of St John Lateran, approved the Franciscan rule and blessed Francis and his companions.
That rule has not survived, except in its revised form
dating from 1221, and it is full of Scripture. Here is an
extract from the first chapter.

> The Rule and life of these brothers is this, namely
> to live in obedience, in chastity, and without any-
> thing of their own, and to follow the teaching and

the footsteps of Our Lord Jesus Christ, who says:
'If thou wilt be perfect, go and sell all that thou
hast and give to the poor, and thou shalt have
treasure in heaven; and come, follow Me.'

Francis received the stigmata, the wounds of the
crucified Christ, in 1224. Blind and ill but still full of
joy, at San Damiano where he was being cared for by
St Clare, Francis composed a hymn of praise in which
he called upon all creatures (his brothers and sisters)
to praise their creator. The verse about 'Sister Death'
was added shortly before Francis died:

Most High, omnipotent, good Lord,
To you praise, glory and honour and all benediction.
To you alone, Most High, do they belong,
And there is no one worthy to mention you.
Praised be my Lord,
by means of all your creatures,
and most especially by Sir Brother Sun,
Who makes the day, and illumines us by his light:
For he is beautiful and radiant with great splendour;
And is a symbol of you, God most High.
Praised be my Lord,
by means of Sister Moon and all the stars:
For in heaven you have placed them,
clear, precious and fair.
Praised be my Lord, by means of Brother Wind,
And by means of the air, the clouds,
and the clear sky and every kind of weather,
through which you give your creatures nourishment.
Praised be my Lord, by means of Sister Water:
For she is very useful, humble, precious and chaste.
Praised by my Lord, by means of Brother Fire,
By whom you do illumine the night:

For he is fair and gay and mighty and strong.
Praised be my Lord,
by means of our sister Mother Earth,
Which sustains us and keeps us,
And brings forth varied fruits
with coloured flowers and leaves.
Praised be my Lord,
through those who give pardon for love of you,
And suffer infirmity and tribulation.
Blessed are they who endure all in peace,
For they, O God most High,
will be crowned by you.
Praised be my Lord, through our sister Bodily Death,
From whom no living person can escape.
Woe to those who die in mortal sin!
But blessed are those found in your most holy Will,
For the second death will do them no harm.
Praise and bless my Lord,
And thank him, And serve him with great humility.

On 29 November 1979, Pope John Paul II, at the request of an international ecological institute, declared that St Francis was to be regarded as patron saint of scientists and students who are concerned about the physical well-being of the universe, particularly of planet Earth. Here is an extract from the life of St Francis written by Thomas of Celano:

> It would take too long and be well nigh impossible to gather together and recount all that the glorious Father Francis did and taught while he lived among men. For who could ever describe his great love whereby he was caught up in all things that belong to God? Who would be able to tell of the joy he felt as he contemplated in creatures the

wisdom of the Creator, his power and his goodness? In very truth a marvellous and indescribable
joy would often fill him when he beheld the sun
and gazed at the moon, the stars, and the whole
sweep of the heavens. Oh what simple piety and
pious simplicity!

Even for worms he had great affection because
he had read what was said of the [suffering] Savi-
our: 'I am a worm and not a man' [Psalm 21:27].
Moreover, he would pick them up along the road
and put them in a safe place where they would
not be trodden underfoot. What shall I say of other
lowly creatures? we know that in winter, concerned about the bees lest they die of the cold, he
would prepare honey and good wine for them!
Their remarkable way of working stirred him to
such praise of the Lord that he would often spend
a whole day in such prayer, lauding them and
other creatures of the Lord. Indeed, filled with the
Spirit of God, he did not cease to glorify, praise
and bless the Creator and Lord of all in all the
elements and creatures.

The beauty of the flowers brought him great
delight of soul in their shape and colour and sweet
odour, and thus lifted his heart and soul to him
who is the Flower of Jesse. And when he came
upon a field of flowers, he would preach to them
as though they understood him and would invite
them to praise the Lord. He often did the same in
fields of grain, in vineyards, in the woods, the
while he called on all things, earth and fire, air
and wind, to love the Lord and serve him! Truly,
even then he had attained the freedom of the glory
of the children of God! [Romans 8:1].

A few days before he died, Francis asked to be carried down the hill from Assisi to the Porziuncula, the 'little portion' where he had set up home with his friars. He blessed the city before he died and prayed that it would always be a place of peace. Brother Leo, who helped to wash Francis' body before it was buried, told a Franciscan chronicler, Salimbene of Parma, that Francis truly seemed like a man who had been crucified and taken down from the Cross. Salimbene added, 'Never in the history of this whole world was there anyone other than the blessed Francis on whom Christ imprinted the five wounds in likeness to himself.'

A companion of St Francis, Brother Masseo, once asked him, 'Why does all the world seem to be running after you and wanting to see you and hear you and obey you? You're not a very handsome man. You don't have great learning or wisdom! You're not of noble blood! So why is it that all the world is coming to you?' Francis replied, 'You want to know why after me? Why? Because God did not find a greater sinner than me or one more simple and foolish, and so he chose me because he has chosen the foolish things of the world to bring to naught the noble and great and strong!'

Leonardo Boff writes on the final page of his book on St Francis:

> The Gospel seriousness of Francis is surrounded by lightheartedness and enchantment because it is profoundly imbued with joy, refinement, courtesy and humour. There is in him an invincible confidence in humanity and in the merciful goodness of the Father. As a result, he exorcises all fears and threats. His faith does not alienate him from the world; nor does it lead him into a pure valley of

tears. On the contrary, it transforms him through gentleness and care in land and home for the fraternal encounter, where persons do not appear as 'children of necessity, but as children of joy'. We can dance in the world because it is the theatre of the glory of God and of his children. Francis of Assisi, more than an idea, is a spirit and a way of life.[11]

FOR PRAYER AND REFLECTION

1. As a young man, Francis prayed constantly, 'Lord, what do you want me to do?' You are invited to make the same prayer. Imagine that Jesus answers your prayer by saying (as he said to the blind man at Jericho), 'What do you want me to do for you?' (Mark 10:51). How do you reply?

2. It seemed to the young Francis 'unbearably bitter to see lepers'. Is there anyone or anything that fills you with unbearable bitterness? Offer your bitterness to Jesus on the cross and embrace the person or object in imagination.

3. Imagine that Francis appears to you in a dream. You ask him, 'What is the point of it all?' How does he reply?

4. Pray Francis' *Canticle of the Creatures* and extend it by adding your own verses in praise of God.

5. Two years before he died, Francis wrote with his own hand a blessing for Brother Leo – using Numbers 6:24–26. You are invited to substitute your own name for Leo's and to read it prayerfully:

> May the Lord bless you and keep you;
> may he show his face to you

and have mercy on you.
May he turn his face to you
and give you peace.
The Lord bless you, Brother Leo.

6. Francis used to make this prayer before the crucifix.
You may like to pray it slowly before a reproduction
of the Assisi crucifix or before a crucifix you know:

O most high, glorious God, enlighten the darkness
of my heart and give me a right faith, a certain
hope and a perfect love, understanding and knowledge, O Lord, that I may carry out your holy and
true command.

Julian of Norwich

IN 1981, A YOUNG WOMAN whom I shall call Jane was invited to make contact with me by a mutual friend. Jane was a very disturbed person, physically and psychologically handicapped, in a wheelchair, rejected as a child by her parents. A couple of years after I'd got to know Jane, her doctor discovered that some of her problems were caused by an allergy to milk. A few drops of milk, used for instance in cooking, could send her into the depths of depression. Overwhelmed by the sheer darkness of her life, Jane would give way to self-loathing and despair. She would use a razor blade to slash her own face.

This strange behaviour ensured that Jane who desperately needed friends terrified anyone who got to know her. They didn't know how to cope with her. A person of great intelligence, who had a real gift with words, she remained desperately isolated. Our mutual friend thought that a visit to St Cassian's Centre might be helpful for Jane. But first she had to be assured that she would be welcome. She had to be persuaded to make her own way to Kintbury, since she was not in contact with any of the usual groups of young people who came together.

Jane phoned me, as our friend had suggested, and

asked if she could come to St Cassian's. She had a
small car and she would drive up from the south coast
where she lived and spend the afternoon with me. I
told her she would be welcome. 'When? she asked.
'Why not come next Saturday?' I suggested, and, rather
nervously, she agreed. Saturday came, but there was
no sign of Jane. She phoned on Sunday, saying that she
had wanted to come but had been frightened. I told
her there was nothing to be frightened of, and suggested she might come on the following Saturday.
'Yes,' she said, 'I'll come next Saturday.' But she didn't
arrive. After several similar false starts, she eventually
arrived, but was very anxious not to come into the
house. I helped her get from the driving seat of her car
into her wheelchair, and I pushed her up and down our
drive for an hour or so, enjoying the air of the Berkshire
countryside, and listened to her lively if rather nervous
conversation about herself and her neighbours. I said
very little to her that I can remember, and eventually
(after she had refused to come indoors for a meal) I
helped her into her car and waved goodbye. She said
she would write to me, and that she would come back
again for a longer visit.

I was surprised a few days later to receive a postcard
from her. On it, written in bright green ink, were these
words:

> Dear Damian,
> thank you, thank you, thank you, thank you,
> thank you,
> thank you, thank you, thank you. thank you,
> thank you,
> for showing me that God loves the very me that I
> have so despised.
> Love, Jane.

I still have the card. I refer to it as my 'eucharistic postcard'. What else, with all those 'thank yous'? I was very pleased that, somehow, I had conveyed some good news to Jane. I didn't know how. Somehow God uses us in unexpected ways. It is an astonishing, if comforting, thought.

❆

For this is how God loved the world:
he gave his only Son,
so that everyone who believes in him
   may not perish
but may have eternal life.
For God sent his Son into the world
not to judge the world,
but so that through him
   the world might be saved.
                    (John 3:16–17)

We have recognised for ourselves,
and put our faith in,
   the love God has for us.
God is love,
and whoever remains in love
   remains in God
and God in him.
Love comes to its perfection in us
when we can face
   the Day of Judgement fearlessly,
because even in this world
we have become as he is.
                    (1 John 4:16–17)

If God is for us, who can be against us: Since he did not spare his own Son, but gave him up for the sake of all of us, then can we not expect that with him he will freely give us all his gifts? Who can bring any accusation against those that God has chosen? When God grants saving justice who can condemn? Are we not sure that it is Christ Jesus, who died – yes and more, who was raised from the dead and is at God's right hand – and who is adding his plea for us? Can anything cut us off from the love of Christ – can hardships or distress, or persecution, or lack of food and clothing, or threats or violence; as scripture says

> *For your sake we are being massacred*
> *   all day long,*
> *treated as sheep to be slaughtered?*

No; we come through all these things triumphantly victorious, by the power of him who loved us. For I am certain of this: neither death nor life, nor angels, nor principalities, nothing already in existence and nothing still to come, nor any power, nor the heights nor the depths, nor any created thing whatever, will be able to come between us and the love of God, known to us in Christ Jesus our Lord.

(Romans 8:31–39)

◄━━━►

The essential message of the fourteenth-century spiritual writer, Julian of Norwich, is that God loves us: 'that our life is all based and rooted in love, and without love we cannot live'.

We know very little about Julian. We are not even sure whether 'Julian' was her name. She was born on the Norfolk coast in 1343. She lived a religious life and lived in a small dwelling attached to St Julian's church in Norwich, so she may have acquired the name 'Julian' from this connection. We are not sure when she died: she was still alive in 1413. She lived alone, and led a life of prayer and meditation. She was also available to give spiritual advice to those who came to consult her. She may have been a professed nun, or she may have been a laywoman. The one thing we know about her is that she experienced in one day and one night (8 May, 1373), in the course of a severe illness, a series of remarkable 'revelations' or 'showings', which she describes as 'a revelation of love that Jesus Christ, our endless joy, made in sixteen showings or revelations, in detail'.[12]

After twenty years of meditating on what she had seen in 1373, Julian wrote an account of her revelations in eighty-six chapters. A copy of the manuscript was discovered in Paris by an English Benedictine monk in the mid 1600s. A printed edition was published in 1670. A manuscript of Julian was rediscovered in the nineteenth century. In 1909, a manuscript of a shorter version of her book was discovered. This has twenty-five chapters. Scholars believe that Julian wrote (or, more likely, dictated) this version shortly after the original visions. She describes herself as 'a simple creature that had learned no letter' at the time of the sixteen showings, so it is possible that she learned the necessary skills simply in order to be able to write a more detailed account of her experiences and of the convictions in which she had grown during the years of prayer and meditation. She had no written models to follow, but she writes with great freshness and inspiring simplicity.

Julian's visions were of the suffering Jesus, of 'Our Blessed Lady Saint Mary', of God in all things, of heaven, of the meaning of life, of sin, of God's forgiveness, of her own soul or 'inner self'. In the fifth chapter, she describes, using the image of 'a little thing, the

size of a hazel nut' her vision of the way our Lord's
'simple loving' enfolds everything which exists:

> I saw that he is to us everything that is good and
>   comfortable for us.
>   He is our clothing which for love enwraps us,
>   holds us,
>   and all encloses us because of His tender love,
>   so that He may never leave us.

> And so in this showing I saw that he is to us
>   everything that is good,
>   as I understood it.

> Also in this revelation he showed a little thing,
>   the size of an hazel nut
>   in the palm of my hand,
>   and it was as round as a ball.

> I looked at it with the eye of my understanding and
>   thought:
>   'What can this be?'

> And it was generally answered thus: 'It is all that
>   is made.'

> I marvelled how it could continue,
>   because it seemed to me it could suddenly have
>   sunk into nothingness because of its
>   littleness.
> And I was answered in my understanding:
>   'It continueth and always shall, because God
>   loveth it;
>   and in this way *everything* hath its being by the
>   love of God.'

And so in chapter 31:

> ... our good Lord replied to all the questions and
>   doubts that I could raise,
>   saying most reassuringly:
>   'I am able to make everything well, and
>   I know how to make everything well, and
>   I wish to make everything well, and
>   I shall make everything well; and
>   thou shalt see for thyself that all manner of thing
>   shall be well.'

Like St Paul's vision of life, Julian's way of thinking
is full of optimism. Yet, when she was writing, England was plagued by a succession of ills: the Hundred
Years' war with France (from 1338); several epidemics
of the Black Death (in the course of which over one
third of the population of Norwich was wiped out);
bouts of famine which led to the Peasants' Revolt;
severe repression of 'heretics', several of whom were
burned to death in Norwich, not far from the hermit's
cell where Julian lived. Yet, Julian has no doubts about
God's assurance to her that 'all shall be well'. She
wrestles (in chapter 32) with the attempt to reconcile
sin and the church's teaching of possibility of dam-
nation with our Lord's promise that 'all shall be well'.

> At this sight I marvelled greatly, and looked at our
>   Faith, marvelling thus: our Faith is based in
>   God's word, and it is part of our Faith that we
>   believe that God's word shall be preserved in all
>   things,

> and one point of our Faith is that many creatures
>   shall be damned ...

and many on earth who die outside of the Faith of
Holy Church . . .
all these shall be damned to hell without end, as
Holy Church teaches me to believe.

Given all this, it seemed to me that it was
impossible that all manner of thing would be
well as our Lord showed at this time;
and in regard to this, I had no other answer in any
showing of our Lord God except this:
'What is impossible for thee is not impossible for
me.
I shall preserve my word in all things,
and I shall make everything well.'

Thus I was taught by the grace of God that I should
steadfastly keep myself in the Faith as I had
interpreted it before, and *also* that I should
firmly believe that everything shall be well as
our Lord showed at the same time; because
this is the Great Deed that our Lord shall do,
in which Deed he shall preserve his word in
everything and he shall make well all that is
not well.
But what the Deed shall be, and how it shall be
done, there is no creature beneath Christ that
either knows it or shall know it until it is done.

The final chapter of Julian's account brings together
in a moving passage the conviction that the Lord's
meaning is love:

From the time that it was shown, I desired
frequently to know what
our Lord's meaning was. And fifteen years after (and

more) I was answered in spiritual understanding,
saying thus:
'Wouldst thou know thy Lord's meaning in this
thing?
Be well aware:
   love was his meaning.
Who showed it thee? Love.
What showed he thee? Love.
Why did he show it thee? For love.

Keep thyself in that love and thou shalt know and
     see more of the same,
but thou shalt never see nor know any other thing
     therein without end . . .

In our creation we had a beginning,
but the love in which he created us was in him
     from without beginning,
and in this love we have our beginning.

And all this we shall see in God without end,
     which may Jesus grant us. Amen.

FOR PRAYER AND REFLECTION

1. Why do you think the revelations of Julian of Norwich have proved to be particularly attractive to readers in the late twentieth century?
2. Julian's vision of love as God's meaning constitutes her answer to the question, 'What is the point of it all?' Her writing shows that she is unable to reconcile the reality of evil and the Church's teaching about the possibility of hell with her conviction that, in God's providence '*all* shall be well'. Yet she is not disturbed by this. We saw, in the extract from

chapter 32, that, without understanding how the two beliefs could be reconciled, she was determined to affirm that 'all shall be well'. Do you find her vision convincing? If so, why? If not, why not?

3. In contrast with the more commonly used masculine language used by theologians, Julian often speaks of God and Christ in feminine language as 'our Mother'. For instance, in chapter 58, writing of the Trinity, Julian writes: 'I saw that the Second Person, who is our Mother in essence, that same dearworthy Person has become our Mother in flesh.'

   Do you think of God in exclusively masculine or feminine imagery? What difference does it make?

4. Use Julian's vision of the hazel nut to contemplate our world, made, loved and sustained by God. In imagination try to include in the scene any fears or anxieties which haunt you. Pray for God's gift of peace in your life. Ask God to bless planet earth and all creation.

Sharing the Darkness

◆━━━▶

THIS CHAPTER FOLLOWS a rather different pattern to the others in this book. It contains two poems and an explanatory comment, reflections on experience of failure in my ministry as a Brother.[13] I shall start with a Scripture passage on which I was led to meditate as a result of meetings with two young people I knew in the 1970s. Tony and Clive are two of the young people who influenced my life more deeply than they will ever know. They live on in my memory – not as kids I tried to teach, but as fellow-pilgrims, sharing the road, stepping into my life, then disappearing down alternative ways. They were more than 'pupils' – they were, in C. P. Snow's evocative phrase, 'strangers and brothers', who raised the question 'what's the point of it all?' My relationship with them was that I was in the position of 'teacher'. But who was teaching whom? I know that I failed to teach them very much. They rejected what I offered them, but they taught me a lot about myself. Any reader who is or has been a teacher may recognise the experience.

First the Scripture passage, the story of an invitation offered by Jesus to a rich young man, an invitation which was turned down in an incident which left the unnamed young man, (and possibly Jesus himself), feeling sad:

He was setting out on a journey when a man ran up, knelt before him and put this question to him, 'Good master, what must I do to inherit eternal life?' Jesus said to him, 'Why do you call me good? No one is good but God alone. You know the commandments: You shall not kill; You shall not commit adultery; You shall not steal; You shall not give false witness; You shall not defraud; Honour your father and mother.' And he said to him, 'Master, I have kept all these since my earliest days.' Jesus looked steadily at him and he was filled with love for him, and he said, 'You need to do one thing more. Go and sell what you own and give the money to the poor, and you will have treasure in heaven; then come, follow me.' But his face fell at these words and he went away sad, for he was a man of great wealth.

Jesus looked round and said to his disciples, 'How hard it is for those who have riches to enter the kingdom of God!' The disciples were astounded by these words, but Jesus insisted, 'My children,' he said to them, 'how hard it is to enter the kingdom of God! It is easier for a camel to pass through the eye of a needle than for someone rich to enter the kingdom of God.' They were more astonished than ever, saying to one another, 'In that case, who can be saved?' Jesus gazed at them and said, 'By human resources it is impossible, but not for God: because for God everything is possible.'

(Mark 10:17–27)

W. B. Yeats, in one of his last poems called 'The Municipal Gallery Revisited', wrote of a visit to the Dublin art gallery which displays the portraits of his friends and contemporaries: 'Around me the images of 30 years,' with all the hopes and disappointments of a lifetime – a 'hallowed place where my friends' portraits hang'.

For each of us, the memory is a 'hallowed place', haunted by the images of people who have disturbed our lives with words and actions which have had a decisive impact on our personal development.

For me, as a Christian, in search of God, the faith-journey takes me into 'hallowed places' where I explore my memories with the eyes of my imagination. How else can I perceive the formative images? This is an aspect of my prayer. It is unpredictable and painful. It is hard to share, but, from time to time, I am moved to write poetry. This happened twice and I feel called to share both the poems and the experiences which they represent. And here I am writing of Tony and Clive. I wonder what they'd think of all this!

The relationships on which I reflect in the two poems were difficult and testing and incomplete. I met Tony in 1970 when he was 14. I taught him English and Religion for four years. He was intelligent, independent and thoughtful. He could be creative, but did not always choose to be. The older he grew, the more dreamy and introspective he became. He often failed to produce the written work assigned. Teachers described him as lazy, but one or two of us knew him better. He was a voracious reader, for instance, who alarmed his parents by bringing home stacks of library books – huge tomes of Freud and Jung, and more recent books on psychology or anthropology. ('Are all these books maddening and disturbing him?' his father once asked me. 'Or is he really mad and trying to understand himself?')

Tony could be very friendly and witty, but often he would remain aloof, locked in his own world. In Form 6, he attended school irregularly, and he experimented with soft drugs. There were times when he would roam round with more active 'normal' kids, but I suspect he was a mystery to them. He was erratic and unpredictable. Sometimes he'd be cynical and irksome in discussion; at other times he'd be the model sixth-form student, asking searching questions, reading anything you'd set before him, producing lengthy complex essays, catching up on past omissions, asking for private tutorials – then losing interest, slumping, truanting.

I liked Tony, wanted to help, appreciated the trust he placed in me. We had several long personal discussions. His father, thinking I had some influence over the boy, came to see me more than once, sharing his anxiety, asking advice. I knew that Tony had been having a stormy time with his parents over problems of schoolwork, irregular attendance, lack of interest in a career, girlfriend troubles, drinking ... Confrontations became rows and were followed by long periods of silence – all the usual problems of relationship between parents and teenagers, but magnified, experienced more intensely.

Looking back, I see that it would have been impossible to find a solution. At school, the inevitable happened: Tony, who could have achieved a Grade One pass in English, failed this and his other advanced level examinations. He wrote over 20 pages in the first English exam, but answered only two of the five questions required. He arrived late for his history exam, strolling nonchalantly into the classroom, apparently unconcerned, but wide-eyed and pale. I heard that on leaving school, he had a couple of dead-end jobs and was sacked from them.

This happened nearly twenty years ago. From time to time I think about Tony and pray for him. He would smile, I think, to hear this. He'd long ago rejected Christ and the church, though he was always deeply interested in religious and spiritual questions. Other kids objected, mocked, or yawned in bored indifference; sometimes Tony pretended to, but he knew better. He seemed destined for failure. What a dreadful waste, but what could I or anyone do? With regret I learned to accept the hard lesson so beautifully expressed by C. Day Lewis, reflecting on his son:

> Selfhood begins with a walking away
> And love is proved in the letting go.

I had to let Tony go. I loved and respected him. I think of him whenever I read the account of the rich young man: how Jesus 'looked steadily at him and loved him', and then watched him 'walk away sad, for he was a man of great wealth.' I used to wonder how Tony would use the enormous wealth of his intelligence and sensitivity.

I heard he had some dangerous encounters with drugs, but that would be only a phase. For all I know, he has settled down to a steady job and a conventional marriage. By chance, some years ago, I met him in a pub with his wife. We had a drink together and exchanged small talk. I didn't tell him I had written a poem about him. He asked if I were still a Brother. Anyway, Tony, you never left my life, and one evening, more than twelve years ago, when I was meditating on my own journey of faith, and of those who have accompanied me in its various stages, your familiar

face loomed up out of my memory and I saw those big
eyes smiling. And then the poem came, as for once I
had the time to wrestle with the words and write it
down.

For Tony

Your eyes still haunt me, and your curling mouth
Armed with some question, smiling in disbelief.
I tried to help you, failed, and let you go –
I had to – but you never left my heart.
I often wonder what you're asking now
(Still overturning someone's apple cart?) –
If with that drugged intelligence, you became
What you once promised – or just drifted on the
    stream
Of your unconscious destiny: to doubt,
To keep on doubting. Your anxious father tried
To help, came to me by night, feared you'd find out.
That was the end, I think. And every word
Of those introspective questions, tortuous paragraphs
Of argument, half-baked views you'd read or heard,
Seemed all in vain. We never said goodbye.
I watched you wander away. That night I cried.

Clive was a slight, bright-eyed boy who came to our
retreat-centre in Kintbury when he was sixteen. He
was a strange figure, who remained on the fringes of
what was happening. Others responded to the warmth
and welcoming atmosphere, the informality and
relaxed approach; they broke through their barriers of
shyness, entered into the prayerfulness of the liturgy,
were touched by the Spirit, accepted the invitation to
open up and share friendship. I watched them grow
(almost visibly) in faith. But Clive remained on the

fringe, curled up on a chair, alert, looking into the circle from the outside. His eyes glinted, with detachment rather than with resistance. He refused communion, said nothing when everyone else took turns to pray. He was silent, for the most part, during discussions; enigmatic, perhaps cynical, definitely an outsider, an observer. He always carried a leather bag, which contained his expensive camera and its attachments. Clive was a photographer, specialising in black and white blow-ups. Somehow, that seemed appropriate.

I asked how he was finding the experience and why had he come here. He talked about himself, at first cautiously, then less stiffly. He was, he said, 'interested' in what was happening to the others, but remained untouched by it all – because he was an atheist. Religion fascinated him, especially Buddhism. He had no time for Christianity or the Church, which was ineffectual, hypocritical, shallow. He was intrigued by what was happening here to his mates, who were (with one exception) acquaintances rather than friends. Nearly all of them, to his surprise, had 'let go' – they were obviously experiencing what I called the power of Christ. For them, it was an experience of faith. Not for Clive. For him it was a sociological phenomenon, an experience of religion and its strange assertive grip over people's behaviour. He was puzzled and fascinated, intellectually, by what was going on. It was an enigma – a phenomenon to be observed, considered, recorded, perhaps even photographed, then analysed and explained.

The next time his school arranged a visit to our centre, Clive was with the party – and the next time. His curiosity and appetite were insatiable, but there was no sign of a conversion. We spoke together often, exchanged news on an intellectual level. Skilfully, he resisted my efforts to go deeper, to help him make the painful transition from the head to the heart. He disagreed with me endlessly, scrutinised and challenged every statement, played games with words. We became old friends, like sparring partners rehearsing old familiar fights, occasionally stumbling across a new skill, a refined technique, an intellectual insight.

I felt that Clive had been deeply wounded. I suspected some sort of family problem. I wanted to respect his freedom, his silences, but also to hear and respond to his cry for help. Why did he keep returning here? I encouraged him to share his feelings as well as his ideas. Always he resisted. I respected his rights. It was a living restatement of the old truism, conveyed vividly in the famous painting by Holman Hunt, that some doors open only from the inside. If this one opened from the outside, I had no key.

One Saturday evening, just before starting a prayer-vigil with the group, I told Clive that I was going to pray for him (if he would like me to), and that afterwards, quietly, I'd like to pray with him. Would he agree?

The old cautious, defensive look came back into his eyes. He said he would think about that during the prayer-service, and then tell me later. The prayer was to culminate in a simple Eucharist. Earlier that day, each participant had been invited to offer some symbol of himself, as a preparation for the Eucharist. Everyone had co-operated enthusiastically, except Clive, of course. Now he surprised me.

'This is what I wanted to offer,' he said, 'but I didn't want to offend.'

He handed me a large pencil-drawing, beautifully shaded – almost three dimensional – like a fine, cleverly lit black and white photograph. He had drawn an earthenware chalice, like the one we used; but embedded in its rim was a huge, sharp kitchen knife. The chalice had been almost smashed by the force of the impact, but it had remained intact. From the point where the blade was held fast, a black zigzag lightning crack ran down the side of the cup. It was a drawing of extraordinary power.

'That's me!' he said.

'Which of them is you?' I replied. 'The chalice or the knife?'

He looked startled – began to speak – then stopped.

He came to me afterwards and we talked into the early hours. He didn't reveal everything, but he opened his door wide enough for me to see the pain: his parents' separation, the hatred and the bitterness, his resentment against life, school, women, God. He was still very cautious about my offer to pray with him, but he agreed. His one close friend joined us. Clive listened while I prayed aloud. I had a picture of Lazarus in the tomb and I heard Jesus' shout, commanding his dead friend to come out. I prayed Jesus' words to the onlookers: 'Untie him – let him go free.'

Clive was moved. God seemed close to us. And yet . . .

I wanted Clive to pray in his own words, and first to forgive the people who had hurt him, that he in turn might be forgiven. He was silent for a long time – tried to stammer out some words; but his heart was not with them. He had certainly experienced God's power; for the first time he recognised that he was the half-shattered chalice rather than the knife. But there was still some resistance – not aggression, but a lot of fear.

We ended quietly. The next day he made an ambiguous public reference to the experience, intended for my ears. He had distanced himself. He talked of 'religious con-men who try to trick you into believing'. That hurt me. It was a wounding blow to my pride. I accepted it as a strong reaction, and looked forward to a future meeting, another 'close encounter'.

Some months later, his school organised another visit to our centre. Clive did not come. His friends told me he had intended to, but lost his nerve and made some excuse. Another disappointment for me. Who was the chalice now?

In fact, Clive paid one more visit, but it was brief and superficial. I've not seen him since. He went to university and we lost contact. The next move is his. I pray for him, and sometimes I look at his strange, disturbing drawing. And I wonder about myself.

When I talk of my 'sharing the darkness', Tony's darkness, Clive's darkness, I mean it. I'm not being rhetorical. I have a real sense of failure. You see, I feel unable to share my deepest self, with anyone, and yet I am so moved when others take me into their confidence and develop a relationship in faith and love. These poems have grown out of disappointment and longing, out of a self-doubt and uncertainty, and also out of the hope implicit in the shattering relationships like those I've had with Tony and Clive. These young people have taught me so much, because they've made me ask myself some fundamental questions. I wanted to 'untie them and let them go free', but I discovered my own weakness, my inability to untie not only their knots but also my own. Of course I've had some immensely joyful and enriching experiences with young people, but these do not render the others invalid. The whole process tells me something about the dynamic nature of faith as an ever-deepening, ever-surprising relationship with God and my fellow human beings, especially the young.

I think of Peter professing his love for Jesus, each assurance of personal love followed by a call to feed the lambs and look after the sheep. What this will involve for Peter, for me, and I suspect for anyone who engages in the uncertain and compelling journey of faith, is a very special kind of frustration, one which is particularly trying for teachers, leaders, strong personalities, who want always to lead and who find it painful to be led. Jesus used an expressive metaphor:

> In all truth I tell you,
> when you were young
> you put on your own belt
> and walked where you liked;
> but when you grow old
> you will stretch out your hands
> and somebody else will put a belt round you
> and take you where you would rather not go.
>
>   (John 21:18)

These young men led me 'where I would rather not go', but where I am not sorry to have gone. These experiences of failure have made me realise that I cannot live my vocation to accompany the young in their search for faith unless I really share their darkness and take the frightening plunge into their lives – as they have plunged into mine, creating echoes which still resound, disturbing my private peace and my professional complacency. So I grow in faith. And somewhere, in the midst of it all, is the incarnate God who shares our darkness, turning it into light. I dedicated this poem to Clive.

'All we are called to do is love.'
For one afraid to live alone
That's easy talk! The language failed
To probe its way through skin and bone
Into your heart. You laughed aloud.
The echoes still resound in me,
Shaping the landscape of a dream:
Your dark eyes smile defiantly.

I've searched for gestures. How to prove
I'm chosen to bear witness to
Compulsive metaphors: to save
Drowning children who scream to know
If they are loved? That 'if' appals
Me, when I hesitate to dive
Into dark waters swirling below,
To snatch from death, restore to life.

I fear the dazzling waterfall's
Attendant dangers and delights,
Where all the wounded dreamers go.
I long for other ways to show
Concern for you. They're not enough!
Echoes resound, ambitions live:
All I am called to do is love,
To plunge, to rescue, to forgive –

And be forgiven too, for I,
When stripped of shallow laughter, stand
Naked and scared, haunted by doubts
Not even you would understand.
We share the darkness. Oh, may all
The stones which block both hearts be rolled
Away, to reveal the love I knew
Mere words would not make flesh for you.

FOR PRAYER AND REFLECTION

1. My reflections on Tony and Clive contain refer-
   ences to three Scripture passages: the story of Jesus
   and the rich young man (Mark 10: 17–22); the rais-
   ing of Lazarus (John 11:1–54); the post-resurrection
   meeting between Jesus and Simon Peter (John
   21:1–19).

   You are invited to read each of these passages,
   slowly and meditatively. Do you see any of them
   as relevant to yourself and your life? Does either of
   them recall any meeting or experience you have
   had? Does either of them help you to see what is
   the point of it all?

2. Reflect for some time on any experience of failure
   you have known. What did you learn from the
   experience? Where was God in the experience? How
   can an experience of failure help us to grow?

3. Your life has probably included meetings with
   people who have disturbed your peace – as my
   relationship with Tony and Clive disturbed me. In
   reflecting on Paul's letter to the Philippians, we
   read of his prayer that 'the peace of God which is
   beyond our understanding' would guard their hearts
   and their thoughts. Can you see any advantages in
   experiences which trouble our peace? What have
   you learned about yourself from such disturbance?

4. Spend some time in prayer for peace for an individual, a family or a country which you have known
   where there is now little or no peace.

The Book of Revelation's Answer

ONE OF THE FINAL CHAPTERS of Paul's letter to the Romans contains a beautiful prayer. Paul has been emphasising his favourite theme that Christ's saving mission was directed at both Jews and Gentiles – as foretold by the prophets. For instance, he quotes Isaiah 52 as looking to the future coming of the Messiah, with the words 'The root of Jesse will appear, he who rises up to rule the nations, and in him the nations will put their hope.' And then, as if inspired by that last word, Paul prays for his readers,

> May the God of hope fill you with all joy and peace in your faith, so that in the power of the Holy Spirit you may be rich in hope. (Romans 15:13)

Hope is one of the most important Christian virtues. No treatment of Scripture's answers to the question addressed in this book would be complete without a final reflection on hope. And one of the most powerful depictions of hope in the New Testament is to be found in its final pages, in the Book of Revelation. Many Christians are not attracted to Revelation because its pages seem to be filled with obscure and fearful imagery. John's difficult book of visions has been used repeatedly at various crisis times in history to comment on our world and its calamities, but often not in a spirit of hope. I found myself thinking about the Book of Revelation during a visit to El Salvador in September 1991, when most of the present book had been completed. Of all countries, the tiny troubled land of El Salvador needs hope. And yet its martyrs and its prophets are a sign of hope in the church and the world today.

I was a member of a small group of adult educators visiting El Salvador as part of a study trip organised by CAFOD (Catholic Fund for Overseas Development). During the evening of 27 September, we were taken to meet a group of women of various ages, the 'Monseñor Romero Comité de Co-madres', mothers, wives and sisters whose men-folk have 'disappeared', been kidnapped, imprisoned or assassinated. In danger of their lives, these women meet in mutual support and protest against the injustice which has filled them with so much pain. Our small group's visit coincided with a powercut, and we sat around a candle in the eery darkness listening to our translator's account of the horrific personal experiences being described by these women – experiences of brutal torture and rape at the hands of the military who terrorise so many in that war-torn country where over 8,000 people have disappeared and over 75,000 people have suffered violent deaths since 1975. On 24 March 1980, Archbishop Oscar Romero was assassinated while celebrating Mass. He had told the anguished mothers who had appealed for his support, 'unite together, and in that way you'll be heard'.

We met under his portrait. His prophetic voice still speaks powerfully through these women – a reminder of words he spoke on 27 January, 1980: 'I repeat what

I told you once before when we feared we might be left without a radio station: God's best microphone is Christ, and Christ's best microphone is the church, and the church is all of you. Let each one of you, in your own job, in your own vocation . . . each one in your own place live the faith intensely and feel that in your surroundings you are a true microphone of God our Lord.'[14]

Our eyes were filled with tears as we listened to stories of death-squads, torture, beatings, rape, repression and disappearances – and extraordinary courage and hope. The spirit of the co-madres is that of their patron, Romero, who said one month before he was gunned down, 'Believe me, brothers and sisters, anyone committed to the poor must suffer the same fate as the poor. And in El Salvador we know the fate of the poor: to be taken away, to be tortured, to be jailed, to be found dead.' A week later, Romero declared, 'Lent and Easter are our own, and each people can say so. Christ is a Salvadoran for Salvadorans. Christ has risen here in El Salvador for us, so that with the power of the Spirit we can pursue our own nature, our own history, our own freedom, our own dignity as the Salvadoran people.'[15]

On the day before he died, in a spirit of realism and hope Romero proclaimed the Easter victory of Jesus: 'Just as he will thrive in an unending Easter, so we must accompany him in a Lent and a Holy Week of Cross, sacrifice and martyrdom. As he said, blessed are those who are not scandalised by his Cross . . . Those who have Christian faith and hope know that behind this calvary of El Salvador lies our Easter, our resurrection. That is the Christian people's hope.'[16] These sentiments are exactly those of the Book of Revelation.

I, John, your brother and partner in hardships, in the kingdom and in perseverance in Jesus, was on the island of Patmos on account of the Word of God and of witness to Jesus; it was the Lord's Day and I was in ecstasy, and I heard a loud voice behind me, like the sound of a trumpet, saying, 'Write down in a book all that you see, and send it to the seven churches of Ephesus, Smyrna, Pergamum, Thyatira, Sardis, Philadelphia and Laodicea.' I turned round to see who was speaking to me, and when I turned I saw seven golden lamp-stands and, in the middle of them, one like a Son of man, dressed in a long robe tied at the waist with a belt of gold. His head and his hair were white with the whiteness of wool, like snow, his eyes like a burning flame, his feet like burnished bronze when it has been refined in a furnace, and his voice like the sound of the ocean. In his right hand he was holding seven stars, out of his mouth came a sharp sword, double-edged, and his face was like the sun shining with all its force.

When I saw him, I fell at his feet as though dead, but he laid his right hand on me and said, 'Do not be afraid; it is I, the First and the Last; I am the Living One, I was dead and look – I am alive for ever and ever, and I hold the keys of death and of Hades. Now write down all that you see of present happenings and what is still to come.

(Revelation 1:9–19)

In this first chapter, John proclaims, ' "I am the Alpha and the Omega", says the Lord God, who is, who was, and who is to come, the Almighty,' and then describes the vision he saw during his imprisonment on the convict-island of Patmos. Written to encourage

persecuted Christians during a time of Roman persecution, Revelation uses the imagery of many books
of the Bible to offer hope to God's people and to assure
them of eventual salvation and triumph. John's vision
of the Risen Christ 'alive for ever and ever', with power
over death for all who believe in him, fills the writer
with fear. And yet Jesus' message is 'Do not be afraid;
it is I, the First and the Last; I am the Living One.' The
words recall the Easter message given to the women at
the tomb (Mark 16:6, Matthew 28:5–7, Luke 24:4–7),
as well as in John's Easter narratives explored in an
earlier chapter.

John's prophetic words to the seven representative
churches named contain warnings against infidelity,
weakness, sin and lukewarmness (chapters 2 and 3),
but the underlying message is one of hope and encouragement. John assures his readers that when the overall meaning of history is revealed, in spite of all the
suffering and injustice it has contained, the conclusive
triumph of Christ's resurrection will set everything in
perspective. Suffering and death will be wiped out,
injustice will be overthrown, a new heaven and a new
earth will transform our understanding:

> Then I saw a new heaven and a new earth; the
> first heaven and the first earth had disappeared
> now, and there was no longer any sea. I saw the
> holy city, the new Jerusalem, coming down out of
> heaven from God, prepared as a bride dressed for
> her husband. Then I heard a loud voice call from
> the throne, 'Look, here God lives among human
> beings. He will make his home among them; they
> will be his people, and he will be their God, God-
> with-them. He will wipe away all tears from their
> eyes; there will be no more death, and no more

mourning or sadness or pain. The world of the past has gone.

(Revelation 21:1–4)

The Book of Revelation reminds us that any view of the present world which lacks a future perspective of hope is not a Christian view. Circumstances may force people in countries like El Salvador to cry out in anguish 'What's the point of it all?', but the courage, faith and love which grow out of the mutual support they provide for one another is the fruit of the spirit of the risen Christ – in whose power, as Paul wrote, they are rich in hope.

To meet the courageous mothers of El Salvador was for me a translation of the ancient words of the Book of Revelation into flesh. They helped me to understand the meaning of the graffiti I saw on many walls in San Salvador: 'Mons Romero vive' – 'Monsignor Romero lives', because the risen Christ lives. Christ has died, Christ is risen, Christ will come again. Christ is our peace, Christ is our hope.

FOR PRAYER AND REFLECTION

1. My visit to El Salvador in 1991 renewed my sense of hope. Many aspects of it sickened me and distressed me, but the overall effect was that my faith, hope, love and joy were strengthened. Can you point to the effect of a similar experience in your life?

2. Of the many passages of Scripture which this book has tried to open for you, which passage gives you most hope? Can you think of someone with whom you might share this passage – and this hope? Think

about how you might do it and ask God to fill you
with strength.

3. Read slowly Paul's prayer for the Romans:

    May the God of hope fill you with all joy and
    peace in your faith, so that in the power of the
    Holy Spirit you may be rich in hope.

    (Romans 15:13)

    Pray this prayer for your family and friends, think-
    ing of them individually and picturing their faces.
    Pray it especially for anyone you know whose situ-
    ation is apparently hopeless. Linger on each word.
    Pray it for yourself, replacing 'you' by 'me' and 'I'.

4. Read slowly this extract from the homily preached
    by Archbishop Romero at Mass just before he was
    gunned down:

    'God's reign is already present on our earth in
    mystery. When the Lord comes, it will be brought
    to perfection.'[17] That is the hope that inspires
    Christians. We know that every effort to better
    society, especially when injustice and sin are so
    ingrained, is an effort that God blesses, that God
    wants, that God demands of us.

5. What is the hope that inspires you? How does that
    hope motivate your actions and your outlook? By
    whom and when is it renewed?

References

1. Vatican II, *Gaudium et Spes*, Pastoral Constitution on the Church in the World Today, article 31 from Norman Tanner, *Documents of the Ecumenical Councils*, vol. II (Sheed and Ward and Georgetown University Press 1990).
2. *Gaudium et Spes*, 3.
3. *Gaudium et Spes*, 4.
4. The New Jerusalem Bible (Darton, Longman and Todd 1985), pp. 755–6.
5. John Hull, *Touching the Rock: an experience of blindness* (SPCK 1990).
6. Ibid., p. 48.
7. Ibid., pp. 52–3.
8. *Gaudium et Spes*, 31.
9. Quoted by Eberhard Bethge in his edition of Bonhoeffer's *Letters and Papers from Prison* (SCM Press 1953).
10. *The Testament of Saint Francis*, trans. Ignatius Brady OFM in *The Writings of Saint Francis of Assisi* (Edizione Porziuncola, Assisi 1983).
11. Leonardo Boff, *Saint Francis: a model for human liberation*, (SCM Press 1982).
12. Fr John-Julian, *A Lesson of Love* (Darton, Longman and Todd 1988). The subsequent quotations are taken from this translation.
13. First published in *Word in Life* (May 1979).
14. J. R. Brockman SJ, *The Violence of Love* (Collins 1989), p. 222.

15. Ibid., p. 231.
16. Ibid., p. 241.
17. *Gaudium et Spes*, 39.